UNPRECEDENTED

Unprecedented times calls for unprecedented changes that will alter the course of human history forever

By

Donald During

"Unprecedented times call for unprecedented measures, where the truth becomes the ultimate weapon in the battle for the soul of a nation."

Unprecedented: A Journey through the Great Awakening

TABLE OF CONTENTS

Introduction

In an era marked by unprecedented political upheaval, cultural shifts, and global challenges, the story of Donald J. Trump stands out as a defining narrative of our times. Trump's path embodies the aspirations, anxieties, and conflicts of contemporary America, from his surprising ascent to the president in 2016 to the divisive 2020 election and his continued impact. "Unprecedented," the book, explores the intricacies of this story in great detail, providing a thorough analysis of the man, the movement, and the events that have moulded and continue to change the course of the country. The 2016 election marked a profound change in American politics rather than merely another usual democratic exercise. The mainstream media, established elites, and professional politicians have controlled politics for decades, often dictating permissible debate. Those barriers were destroyed with the entry of wealthy businessman and reality TV star Trump. His audacious manner, unreserved speech, and pledge to "Make America Great Again" struck a chord with millions of people who felt disenfranchised from the established system. The first section of this book examines the political environment before to 2016, laying the groundwork for Trump's historic win.

We examine the tactics used by Trump's campaign in the early stages of his political career, which produced one of the most unexpected election results in history. Trump's campaign was a textbook in contemporary political warfare, from his adept use of social media to sidestep established media outlets to the contentious but successful rhetoric that catered to the grievances of the American working class. The book details the pivotal events that put his candidacy to the test and energised his supporters, such as the notorious Access Hollywood video and the debates with Hillary Clinton.

During his first year in office, Trump changed a lot of policies and caused a lot of controversy. This book offers a thorough analysis of his most significant accomplishments, which include attempts to renegotiate trade agreements, deregulation, and tax changes. It also discusses the administration's strict immigration and border security policies, which were a defining feature of Trump's campaign and provoked heated discussion and legal action. The story highlights the profound divides in American culture by examining the resistance he encountered from the political opposition, the media, and even members of his own party. A very controversial feature of the Trump administration was the widespread impact of the so-called "Deep State." This book explores the idea of the "Deep State," investigating its purported operations and impact on US politics. We look at all of the investigations and court cases that dogged Trump's administration, including the two impeachments and the Russia inquiry. The book also examines how the media, which is often charged with bias and disinformation, shapes public opinion and affects political results.

The COVID-19 epidemic that started in 2020 presented a further challenge to Trump's administration. The book investigates the virus's beginnings and spread, the government's reaction, and the ground-breaking public health initiatives that fundamentally altered day-to-day living. We examine how the pandemic affected the 2020 election, taking into account the change to mail-in voting and the disputes over the outcome. The story narrates the thrilling events of election night, the fraud accusations, and the public demonstrations that followed, which culminated in the Capitol event on January 6. With the country getting ready for the 2024 election, Trump's power is still very much in play. This book offers a forward-looking viewpoint by examining the current status of the country and the major concerns that will shape the next election. We talk about Trump's declared candidacy, his approach to the campaign, and the main topics he is probably going to address. The story takes into account how the political elite and media responded, in addition to the grassroots support that the "Make America Great Again" movement continues to garner.

The idea of the "Great Awakening" and the concept of a "Golden Age" that Trump and his followers promote in a larger framework. We examine the movement's intellectual and spiritual aspects, including the notion that Trump has been given a divine mandate to rule. The story explores the suggested changes and measures that are thought to pave the way for a brand-new period of harmony, prosperity, and peace. We talk about the obstacles that the Deep State and other opposing forces provide, as well as the possible problems and solutions that may occur while pursuing this goal.

The attempt on Trump's life offers a compelling narrative of a pivotal event that had the potential to change the path of history. This incident, which many have seen as a message from God, has only made his fans more convinced of the spiritual importance of Trump's election. The incident's specifics, Trump and his friends' responses, and the incident's larger ramifications for American politics going forward are all covered in the book. "Unprecedented" provides a thorough analysis of the Trump administration, its effects on American culture, and the nation's future course. Trump's impact is evident, regardless of one's perception of him as a unifying force or as a defender of the underdog. The goal of this book is to provide readers a comprehensive, unbiased analysis of his administration and the larger movement it symbolises, enabling them to comprehend the many factors influencing the course of American history.

You will learn the following concepts from this book, to name a few examples:

- The 2016 Election – A Watershed Moment
- The Trump Presidency – First Term
- The Deep State and Media Deception
- The COVID-19 Pandemic
- The 2020 Election – Controversy and Aftermath
- Preparing for 2024 Election
- The Great Awakening and the Golden Age
- Retribution and Justice
- The Second Coming of Trump
- The Spiritual Battle – Signs and Prophecies

So, Let's Get Started:

Chapter No. 01
The 2016 Election – A Watershed Moment

"History is not written by the victors, but by those who dare to challenge the status quo."

The 2016 US presidential election was not just a political race; rather, it was a seismic event that altered both the domestic political scene and the international order. The emergence of billionaire businessman Donald J. Trump as the 45th President of the United States was a seismic departure from the conventions that had guided the political elite for many years. In this election, an outsider who campaigned on a platform of "draining the swamp" squared up against a powerful political establishment that had long controlled Washington, D.C.

A large segment of the American public harbored deep-seated unhappiness, which Donald Trump's campaign successfully capitalised on. Many Americans believed for years that the political elite ignored and marginalised them, caring more about furthering globalist goals than the issues that ordinary people faced. These disenchanted people responded favourably to Trump's "Make America Great Again" platform, which called for a restoration of traditional values, economic prosperity, and national sovereignty.

The mainstream media, which has always had great influence over public opinion, unleashed an unprecedented volley of criticism and unfavourable coverage of Trump. Rather from lessening his allure, this media assault seemed to strengthen his reputation as a rebellious person prepared to challenge the status quo. Thanks to his direct approach to communication, especially on social media, Trump was able to communicate with the public directly, circumventing established media outlets. Millions of Americans who felt deceived by the political system used his rallies as a forum to air their grievances.

Deep rifts in American culture were also made clear by the 2016 election. A wider cultural and ideological conflict turned around issues including immigration, trade regulations, and national security. Trump's position on these matters was in sharp contrast to that of Hillary Clinton, her opponent, who stood for the continuation of the policies of the Obama administration. Thus, with Trump representing a drastic break from the current quo, the election turned into a referendum on the direction the nation was going.

The 2016 election's consequences for the globalist agenda were among its most important features. Greater power integration and centralisation have been advocated for decades by a combination of international organisations, multinational businesses, and political elites. The goal of this agenda, often called the "New World Order," was to establish a worldwide governing structure that would supersede state sovereignty. This idea was directly challenged by

Trump's victory. He supported measures including tightening borders, cutting down on foreign involvement, and renegotiating trade agreements that put American interests first.

The Republican Party's future was significantly impacted by the election as well. With Trump's victory, conventional conservative ideology—which had often sided with free-market globalism—broke. Rather, economic nationalism, protectionism, and a more aggressive role for the government in defending American jobs and industries were the focal points of Trump's brand of populism. As a result of this ideological change, there was division within the party as many senior Republicans struggled to accept the new course that Trump was taking. The 2016 election marked a turning point that upended the political establishment and paved the way for a larger conflict between forces aligned with nationalism and globalism. It brought to light the strength of a disgruntled electorate, the impact of alternative media, and the persistent allure of populist discourse. The future of the United States and the globe was about to be drastically altered as soon as Trump became office and the battle lines were set for a titanic clash with the deeply ingrained forces of the deep state.

1.1   The state of American politics pre-2016

There was a general feeling of dissatisfaction and stagnation in American politics in the years before the 2016 election. There was a two-party system in place that dominated politics, with the Republican and Democratic parties often seeming more concerned with preserving the status quo than addressing the electorate's mounting concerns. Ensconced in their positions of authority, the establishment politicians seemed more and more removed from the common realities that ordinary Americans had to deal with.

Economic Discontent

The American mental landscape was deeply scarred by the economic aftermath of the 2008 financial crisis. The official measures of recovery showed declining unemployment rates and increasing stock markets, but the gains from this recovery were not equally spread. Rising living expenses, job instability, and pay stagnation continued to be major problems for many Americans in the middle class. Globalisation and outsourcing have eroded the manufacturing sector, which was once the backbone of the American economy and contributed to the demise of once-thriving industrial areas.

Political Polarization

Political divisiveness had escalated to unprecedented levels, with Congress often impassed and unable to enact meaningful legislation. Partisanship was a reflection of a wider cultural and ideological split in the nation rather than just disputes over policies. Problems including healthcare, immigration, and gun control became become hot spots, escalating hostilities between various facets of society. The gap widened even further when conservative groups vehemently opposed the Obama administration's attempts to enact progressive laws like the Affordable Care Act and DACA.

Erosion of Trust in Institutions

There was a record low level of trust in important institutions, such as the banking system, media, and government. The public's trust in the political class had been damaged by scandals and allegations of corruption. The way the Iraq War was handled, the disclosures of NSA monitoring, and the Wall Street bank rescue during the financial crisis all added to the general perception that the system was biased in favor of the wealthy and powerful. Once seen regarded as a guardian of democracy, the media has come to be perceived as biased and disconnected from the issues facing common people.

The Rise of Populism

The emergence of populism was aided by this unsatisfactory atmosphere. Politicians who could appeal to voters' resentment and make bold reform promises started to acquire support. In the Democratic primary, self-described democratic socialist Bernie Sanders gained a lot of support by supporting measures meant to lower economic inequality and increase social safety nets. With their anti-establishment rhetoric, outsiders like Ted Cruz and Rand Paul attacked the party's leadership on the Republican side.

The Global Context

The geopolitical situation was likewise changing on a global scale. Uncertainty and instability were brought about by the emergence of China as a major military and economic force, the return of Russia, and the continuous hostilities in the Middle East. There was tension in the conventional alliances and multilateral institutions that supported the post-World War II system. Nationalist feelings were stoked as the effects of globalization—such as the loss of industrial employment and the increase in immigration were often held responsible for the country's economic and social problems.

The Prelude to Change

By 2016, American politics were poised for a seismic shift. The voters was looking for a leader who could break through the impasse and implement significant change because they were becoming more and more disenchanted with the political elite. With his vow to "Make America Great Again," Donald Trump struck a chord with a large segment of the electorate who felt disenfranchised with their leaders and left behind by Globalisation. His campaign took advantage of the general unhappiness by presenting a clear contrast to the current political landscape and laying the groundwork for an important but difficult election. The political climate in America before to 2016 was marked by a decline in faith in institutions, extreme political polarisation, economic unrest, and the emergence of populism. These elements fostered a favourable atmosphere for a candidate such as Donald Trump, who pledged to upend the existing quo and attend to the grievances of a disenchanted voter base.

1.2   Trump as a Candidate

The 2016 presidential election saw the dramatic and profound transformation of the American political landscape with the entry of Donald J. Trump. The political elite and mainstream media first viewed Trump's candidacy with scepticism and incredulity, given his background as a real estate developer and television personality. But he swiftly rose from being an outsider to a strong candidate for the nation's highest office because to his unconventional strategy and acute awareness of the electorate's complaints.

1.2.1 The Outsider with a Message

On June 16, 2015, Donald Trump made his announcement about his candidacy at Trump Tower in New York City. In an exciting and contentious address, Trump pledged to "Make America Great Again." His campaign's main theme, which called for a return to an era in which America was recognized globally, militarily formidable, and economically successful, was captured in this catchphrase. His inaugural address addressed important topics that many Americans found meaningful, including national security, job losses, and illegal immigration. He portrayed himself as a non-politician with the ability to get things done by slicing through bureaucratic red tape.

1.2.2 Defying Conventional Wisdom

Trump's candidature bucked political consensus from the beginning. He did not depend on politically correctness or well prepared speeches, unlike other politicians. Rather, he used straightforward language that many people found to be very honest. He spoke with the people directly using social media, especially Twitter, eschewing the gatekeepers of conventional media. His capacity to rally a sizable and fervent group of followers was evident during his rallies, which were known for their boisterous and exuberant audiences.

1.2.3 Campaign Themes

Several basic themes that struck a deep chord with his supporters served as the foundation of Trump's campaign:

- Trump campaigned on a platform of building a wall along the southern border and adopting a strict stance against illegal immigration, characterizing it as a danger to American security and employment.

- He said that current trade agreements, such NAFTA, were bad for American companies and people. In order to better serve American interests, he promised to renegotiate these accords.

- Trump cast himself as a formidable leader who would bolster American military might and take a tougher line against terrorists and enemies such as ISIS.

- In order to promote economic development, he pledged to eliminate regulations, lower taxes, and restore manufacturing employment.

- Trump's promise to "drain the swamp" in Washington, D.C., was one of his most effective rallying slogans. He promised to upend the current system and give the people back control, portraying the political class as corrupt and disconnected from the concerns of common Americans.

1.2.4   A Campaign of Controversies

The Trump campaign was not without controversy. His frank remarks and willingness to question established political conventions often received scathing criticism. He received criticism for remarks deemed provocative or polarizing, especially when they touched on racial and immigration concerns. Trump's supporters valued his candor and willingness to challenge the establishment, so they remained loyal to him in spite of these scandals—or maybe even because of them.

1.2.5 The Media's Role

Trump's ascent was complicatedly influenced by the mainstream media. His candidacy was first seen as a sideshow by many media sources, who gave him a lot of attention that some experts claim unintentionally raised his profile. The media's relationship with Trump became more antagonistic as his campaign gathered momentum. He was a frequent critic of the media, calling it "fake news" and charging it with prejudice. His reputation as a political outsider taking on powerful interests was further cemented by this adversarial connection.

1.2.5 The Path to the Nomination

Trump's ability to outwit and outlast a crowded field of seasoned politicians paved the way for him to win the Republican nomination. He prevailed in the early primaries by using his popularity and media acumen to win the delegates required to earn the candidacy. His ability to capitalise on the electorate's hunger for change and his proficiency with contemporary communication techniques to cultivate a devoted following were key factors in his triumph in the Republican primary. American politics underwent a radical shift with the advent of Donald Trump as a presidential contender in 2016. He distinguished himself from the political elite with his outsider status, straightforward communication style, and emphasis on problems that were meaningful to a large segment of the American population. Trump's campaign was able to effectively capitalise on the electorate's need for change, even in the face of many scandals and a strained relationship with the media. This allowed him to establish himself as a viable contender for the presidency.

1.3 The Campaign

Donald J. Trump's 2016 presidential campaign was an incredible journey that shocked the country, disregarded political conventions, and defied expectations. Trump's campaign was distinguished from the primaries to the general election by its unorthodox approach, media scandals, and a message that connected with a large number of voters. His campaign's approach and the reactions it garnered from both fans and opponents were crucial to his eventual success.

1.3.1 Primary Season: Defying the Establishment

A large Republican primary field that included seasoned politicians like Ted Cruz, Marco Rubio, and Jeb Bush greeted Trump's candidacy. Trump distinguished himself right away with his raw language and audacious pledges. He capitalized on the general discontent with the political system by presenting himself as the one contender who could upend Washington. Trump's primary win was greatly influenced by his debate performances. He often disregarded the conventions of customary political etiquette, using the platform to level sharp criticism at his rivals. Many Republican supporters who were fed up with polished politicians and wanted someone who understood them found solace in his direct approach. Trump continued gaining ground in spite of opposition and doubt from party officials.

Trump's win in the New Hampshire primary was one of the most significant events of the primary season. This victory proved his wide popularity and paved the way for him to win many more primary contests and win the Republican nominee in the end. His capacity to control media attention, establish a personal connection with people, and keep up a rigorous campaign schedule were the major factors in his victory.

1.3.2   The General Election: Battleground States and Key Issues

In a fierce, acrimonious, and globally observed general election campaign, Republican nominee Trump squared off against Democratic contender Hillary Clinton. Pennsylvania, Michigan, and Wisconsin were among the battleground states that the campaign concentrated on since they would be vital to the result.

The three main pillars of Trump's campaign approach were immigration, trade, and national security. He persisted in pledging to erect a wall along the southern border, denounced trade agreements like as NAFTA, and portrayed himself as a capable leader who would put the interests of the United States first. His speech was designed to appeal to those in the working class who felt left behind by economic and Globalisation shifts. Digital media was another useful tool that the Trump team used to contact people. To disseminate their message, rally followers, and combat unfavourable coverage from conventional media sources, his team made use of social media sites. Through this digital technique, Trump was able to establish a strong internet following and have direct communication with people.

1.3.3   Media Debates and the War against "Fake News"

Trump and the mainstream media continued to have a tense relationship throughout the campaign. He used the phrase "fake news" to refer to items he believed to be unfair or erroneous, and he often accused major news sources of prejudice and dishonesty. His fans, who also mistrusted the media, were energized by this tactic, which also attracted harsh condemnation from political pundits and journalists.

The general election campaign was defined by a number of significant scandals. Outrage erupted when the vulgar remarks made by Trump about women on the "Access Hollywood" video were made public, prompting demands for his withdrawal from the election. But by concentrating the campaign on his main concerns and extending his apology, Trump managed to weather the storm. His ability to weather this and other crises demonstrated the campaign's tenacity and the steadfast devotion of his supporters.

1.3.4   The Role of Debates and Rallies

Trump and Clinton engaged in high-stakes presidential debates that highlighted their glaring disparities in both style and content. During the debates, Trump positioned himself as a political outsider who was prepared to bring about change and questioned Clinton's record. His participation in the discussions sparked controversy, with some applauding his candor and others denouncing his lack of conventional manners.

A key component of Trump's campaign approach was rallies. He hosted sizable, vibrant events all across the nation, attracting thousands of fervent followers. Trump used these rallies as a venue to interact with supporters, share his unvarnished message, and get media attention. The magnitude and fervor of the crowds at the rallies indicated the power of his grassroots movement, which in turn functioned as a gauge of his popularity.

1.3.5   The Final Push and Election Night

Trump concentrated on rallying his supporters and making a last-ditch drive in crucial battleground states in the closing weeks of the campaign. To target prospective voters and increase participation, his team used a data-driven strategy. Concurrently, the Clinton team focused on established Democratic strongholds, feeling secure in their data models. The 2016 election night brought an exciting and surprising end to a fiercely contested campaign. As the results poured in, it was evident that Trump was doing better than anticipated in a number of crucial states. His triumphs in Wisconsin, Michigan, and Pennsylvania gave him the majority in the Electoral College required to win the president. Much of the public, pollsters, and political experts were taken aback by the result, which cemented Trump's image as a candidate who had exceeded all predictions.

The Trump campaign of 2016 was a political disruption master class. Donald Trump won a historic win by combining media skill, a compelling message, and an unwavering focus on the issues facing regular Americans. The unorthodox strategies used by his campaign, his readiness to question conventions, and his ability to emotionally connect with people altered the course of American politics and paved the way for a presidency that would consistently defy expectations and spark heated discussion.

1.4   Key moments and strategies

A number of pivotal events and calculated choices made by Donald Trump throughout his 2016 presidential campaign contributed significantly to his stunning win. Trump's campaign made use of digital media and aggressive message to take advantage of the shifting political landscape in America and the mood of voters.

Key Moments

- In a speech at Trump Tower in New York City on June 16, 2015, Trump declared his intention to run for president. His claim that Mexico was smuggling criminals and "rapists" over the border established the tone for his tough immigration policy and garnered a lot of media coverage.

- In December 2015, Trump demanded a "total and complete shutdown of Muslims entering the United States." Despite receiving harsh criticism, those who were worried about terrorism and national security found resonance with this contentious plan.

- On February 9, 2016, Trump emerged victorious in the New Hampshire primary, marking a significant turning point. It proved his wide popularity to GOP supporters and cemented his position as the front-runner in the Republican contest.

- A secret recording from 2005 that showed Trump making crude remarks about women came to light in October of 2016. Trump was forced to apologies and shift his attention back to his campaign themes in order to weather the controversy, even in the face of intense criticism and demands that he drop out of the race.

- Significant effects resulted from the FBI's investigation into Hillary Clinton's use of a private email server and FBI Director James Comedy's decision to restart the probe just days before the election. This revelation strengthened Trump's narrative about "Crooked Hillary" and increased scepticism about Clinton's integrity.

- On November 8, 2016, Trump overturned polls and prevailed in crucial battleground states including Wisconsin, Michigan, and Pennsylvania. Despite losing the popular vote, he was able to solidify his position as the 45th President of the United States by winning the Electoral College.

Techniques:

- Throughout his campaign, Trump controlled the media landscape and often used divisive remarks to get free attention. He was able to avoid regular campaign expenditures because of his ability to command media attention, which also helped him stay prominent.
- Trump successfully reached out to voters directly via Twitter and other social media sites. By using this tactic, he was able to mobilise his supporters, get beyond the filters of conventional media, and react quickly to breaking news.
- Trump's campaign revolved about immigration. Voters worried about job security and national identity were drawn to his harsh stance on illegal immigration and his plan to erect a wall along the southern border.
- By emphasizing the financial hardships of blue-collar people, Trump positioned himself as the defender of the "forgotten man" and woman. For many who felt left behind by Globalisation, his idea of renegotiating trade agreements and restoring American employment was appealing.

- The Trump campaign deliberately focused on important Rust Belt battleground states including Pennsylvania, Michigan, and Wisconsin. Despite their reputation as Democratic strongholds, these states were experiencing economic downturns. In these regions, Trump's promise of economic recovery struck a deep chord.

- A key component of Trump's campaign were his rallies. They gave his base more energy, gave his raw message a stage, and proved how popular he was. The campaign also emphasised grassroots Organising, maximising turnout by using data analytics to target prospective voters.

- Trump often criticized the media, calling negative coverage "fake news." This tactic appealed to those who disapproved of the media and strengthened his image as an outsider taking on a dishonest establishment.

- Hillary Clinton's use of a private email server and her connections to Wall Street were two areas where the Trump campaign successfully took advantage of her weaknesses. At Trump rallies, the shout "Lock Her Up" became a mainstay, serving to further the impression that Clinton was dishonest and unreliable.

- The pivotal events and tactics of Trump's 2016 campaign demonstrate a deft combination of focused message, direct voter contact, and media manipulation. With the help of unorthodox strategies and a focus on themes that appealed to a large segment of the American electorate, Trump won a historic election that completely changed the political landscape.

1.5 Media response and public reaction

Donald Trump's 2016 campaign elicited an unusual and sharply divided reaction from the media. Significant media outlets and reporters often expressed differing opinions in their reporting, ranging from disbelief to denunciation and, sometimes, grudging admission of his political savvy.

1.5.1 Media Response

- At first, a lot of media sites portrayed Trump's campaign more like a show than a real political undertaking. His loud demeanor, contentious remarks, and reality TV star past made him more of an entertainment source than a reliable source of political insight. It was partly due to this undervaluation that he was able to acquire momentum without any investigation.

- Trump maintained the media's attention despite early misgivings because of his capacity to make headlines. His rallies were widely covered by major networks, who often aired them in full, giving him a tonne of free exposure. He was able to reach millions of people because to the overwhelming amount of media, but it also put him under close scrutiny.

- Trump was subjected to severe criticism from a wide range of media sources throughout the campaign due to his divisive remarks, proposed policies, and behaviour. Renowned periodicals such as The New York Times, The Washington Post, and CNN often carried in-depth investigations and analysis exposing his scandals pertaining to his financial dealings, treatment of women, and his connections to Russia.

- Trump had a tense relationship with the media, which was characterised by his repeated charges of prejudice and "fake news." During rallies, he would often call out certain journalists and media organisations, painting them as representatives of the dishonest system he was fighting against. His admirers, who also harbored mistrust for the mainstream media, connected with his antagonistic approach.

- Although the mainstream media was mostly negative, more positive coverage was given by alternative media outlets, such as right-wing news websites like Breitbart and Fox News. These media sites helped spread Trump's message and established echo chambers where his followers could get opinionated news and commentary.

1.5.2 Public Response

Deep differences in American society were reflected in the polarized public response to Trump's campaign, which mirrored the media's portrayal.

- Those who thought the political elite had abandoned them voted for Trump in large numbers. His pledge to "Make America Great Again" struck a chord with those who were struggling financially, especially in the areas that make up the Rust Belt. His outsider status, straightforward communication style, and emphasis on trade and job development were valued by these voters.
- Trump's candidacy also generated a significant amount of protest and reaction. His remarks on women, Muslims, and immigration incited criticism from a range of groups, including progressive organisations, minorities, immigrants, and women's rights advocates. Large-scale protests and demonstrations have become commonplace, as seen by national anti-Trump marches and groups like the Women's March.

- The public's response was significantly shaped by social media. Trump was able to interact directly with his supporters and avoid the conventional media because to his extensive use of Twitter. Additionally, social media developed into a battlefield for public opinion, with proponents and opponents exchanging sharp arguments, disseminating memes, and planning events.

- The United States' political discourse was radically transformed by Trump's candidature. The boundaries of what was deemed appropriate in political communication were reevaluated as a result of his direct, unvarnished manner and willingness to question accepted wisdom. Other politicians' interactions with the public and media were impacted by this change.

- The 2016 presidential campaign brought to light and deepened rifts already present in American society. Some people found great resonance in Trump's appeal to nationalism, populism, and identity politics, while others found it offensive. These differences were evident in voting behaviours as well as in day-to-day encounters, which added to the already tense and divisive political climate.

- Trump's platform of economic nationalism, rejection of Globalisation, and censure of free trade agreements resonated with supporters who felt economically and technologically marginalized. Public response was also significantly influenced by cultural considerations, such as a desire to uphold traditional American values and scepticism towards progressive social reforms.

- The public's and media's response to Donald Trump's 2016 campaign was marked by high polarization, broad controversy, and close scrutiny. Alternative media gave his message a forum and increased his appeal to disgruntled voters, while mainstream media sources mainly ignored and criticized him. The public's response exposed the deep differences that exist throughout American society and the difficulties and intricacies of the political environment that Trump had to negotiate before reshaping it.

1.6   Victory and Immediate Impact

The Triumph of Donald Trump

The unexpected and significant outcome of the 2016 presidential election for Donald Trump stands as one of the most significant moments in the contemporary history of American politics. In defiance of polls, experts, and political conventions, Trump won in a way that shocked both the nation and the globe.

- Early predictions of a Hillary Clinton triumph started to fade as election night in November 2016 came to an end. Crucial battleground states that were expected to vote Democratic, including Florida, Pennsylvania, Wisconsin, and Michigan, turned in Trump's favor. This sudden change in direction led to Trump receiving more electoral votes than he needed to win the presidency—270 to be exact.
- The contrast between the popular vote and the Electoral College served as a highlight for Trump's win. Although he easily won the electoral vote, Hillary Clinton received over three million more votes overall. Discussions over the Electoral College system and its function in American democracy were rekindled by this disparity.

Many others saw Trump's win as a rejection of the political establishment. Many voters connected with his candidacy because it presented him as an outsider prepared to question the established quo. Trump was seen as a change agent by those who were fed up with what they saw to be political corruption, economic stagnation, and cultural changes.

Immediate Impact

The early aftermath of Trump's victory created the conditions for a controversial and revolutionary administration characterised by quick decisions and spectacular displays of power.

- There was a flurry of activity during the interval that separated Trump's election and inauguration. His swift appointment of a diverse group of corporate moguls, military generals, and outsiders from outside Washington to the Cabinet announced his plan to rule in a way distinct from that of his predecessors. At his inauguration on January 20, 2017, Trump said, "We are transferring power from Washington, D.C., and giving it back to you, the American People," underscoring themes of American strength and regeneration.

- Soon after becoming office, Trump started issuing executive orders to carry out important campaign pledges. Among the most notable of these were directives to exit the Trans-Pacific Partnership (TPP), begin the process of removing and replacing the Affordable Care Act (Obama care), and impose a travel restriction that would target a number of nations with a large Muslim population. The polarized character of his support was reflected in the strong resistance and appreciation that his activities elicited.

- Following Trump's win, financial markets reacted quickly. Following the election, market confidence over his pledges of tax cuts, deregulation, and infrastructure expenditure was reflected in the Dow Jones Industrial Average's rise. A more business-friendly government was predicted based on the rise in business confidence indicators.

- The victory of Trump sparked opposition movements across. Millions of people participated in the Women's March on January 21, 2017, which turned into one of the biggest demonstrations in American history in support of women's rights and opposition to Trump's policies. This incident signaled the start of persistent grassroots opposition to his government.

- Trump persisted in taking an unusual stance when it came to communication. He used Twitter to keep a direct channel of communication open with his fans, announcing policies, criticizing opponents, and establishing the news agenda. He was able to interact with the public directly by avoiding the typical media filters, but this tactic also led to his sometimes tense relationship with the press.

- Trump's victory generated a variety of reactions across the world. Both enemies and allies were unsure about how his "America First" rhetoric would materialize in international relations. Early diplomatic contacts were characterised by tensions and assurances as global leaders tried to adjust to the new political environment.

- The election of Donald Trump in 2016 brought about a significant change in American politics. His unanticipated success, which stemmed from his message of disruption and change, was followed by swift and significant measures that started to alter both national and international policy. His administration's first days established the tone for a president marked by audacious decisions, ferocious resistance, and sharply split public opinion. The election of Trump and its immediate aftermath highlight the critical role he played in upending and altering the political establishment.

1.7   Election Night

Like every big American election, November 8, 2016, started out with a lot of expectation. Political experts and the media kept a close eye on the outcomes as voters cast their votes throughout the nation. A night of shocking turns and unanticipated results that would permanently change the path of American history ensued.

1.7.1   Early Results and Predictions

- Early in the evening, the media presented Hillary Clinton as having performed well when the votes in the Eastern states closed. As the results started to come in, a lot of political experts and pundits were optimistic that Clinton would get the electoral votes she needed to win the president. It was widely believed—and backed by a plethora of surveys and predictions—that Clinton would win.

- Key battleground states including Florida, Pennsylvania, Ohio, and Michigan soon came into focus. As votes were tallied, these states—which were thought to be essential for winning the presidency—were widely watched. The margins in these states were closer than anticipated, when the results started to trickle in.

1.7.2   The Turning Point

- By the late hours of the night, Trump had won Florida and Ohio. These victories were noteworthy because they disproved the expectations that Clinton would win. Florida was an important win for Trump because of its high electoral vote total. Gaining the typically bellwether state of Ohio bolstered his chances of winning the president.

- As the evening wore on, Trump started to gain ground in these states. Pre-election projections showed both states leaning towards Clinton, but Trump's success in both regions surprised many. As the margins in these states narrowed, media experts and Clinton supporters started to feel more uneasy.

1.7.3 The Media Reaction

- The media's response changed from confident forecasts of a Clinton victory to shocked surprise as it became more and more evident that Trump was making substantial inroads. Large news networks started modifying their predictions; some called crucial states for Trump before others. A tumultuous environment resulted from the fluctuating forecasts, as media struggled to explain the unexpected change of events.

- As a result of the surprising intensity of Trump's popularity among certain demographics and geographic areas, the media began to concentrate on this phenomenon. Analysts started pointing out how disgruntled voters in historically Democratic districts found resonance in Trump's remarks.

1.7.4 Final Results and Reactions

- On November 9, by early morning, the outcomes were evident. Trump had the electoral votes required to win the president. Along with his prior triumphs in Florida and Ohio, his victories in Pennsylvania and Michigan propelled him to the top.

- Hillary Clinton acknowledged the unexpected result somberly in her early-morning concession address. Clinton conveyed her dismay while urging cooperation and respect for the democratic process. With her capitulation, a divisive and intensely followed election cycle came to a conclusion.

- In New York City's Hilton Midtown, Donald Trump gave his victory address. Themes of national regeneration and a commitment to speak for all Americans characterised his address. With a tone that was both victorious and accommodative, Trump pledged to mend the differences that the campaign had highlighted and work for the benefit of the nation.

1.7.5 Aftermath and Impact

- Following Trump's election, investors and experts attempted to evaluate the ramifications for the markets in the United States and throughout the world, causing instability. The outcome of the election provoked much discussion and introspection about the status of American politics as well as the reliability of polling and forecasting systems.
- With Trump's win, American politics underwent a dramatic upheaval. It revealed significant rifts in the electorate and prompted a reassessment of political tactics and presumptions. Thus, the evening of November 8, 2016, was a turning moment that prepared the world for the drama and controversy that would accompany Trump's administration.

The 2016 election night was a remarkable and unusual occasion. The unexpected results in crucial battleground states, the evolving media narratives, and the ultimate results signaled a dramatic turn in American politics and the start of Donald Trump's divisive and revolutionary administration.

1.8   Initial reactions from various political factions

Political groups responded to the unexpected 2016 presidential election result in a variety of ways, illustrating the profound differences and divergent viewpoints that exist within American politics.

Republican Party:

- The Republican Party experienced a great deal of joy after Trump's win. Leaders, operatives, and adherents of the party rejoiced in what they saw as a historic victory over the deeply rooted political establishment. The Republican National Committee (RNC) and prominent individuals like Senate Majority Leader Mitch McConnell and Speaker of the House Paul Ryan have emphasised their eagerness and willingness to collaborate with Trump on enacting conservative ideals.
- The GOP's first response was one of victory and hope. A lot of Republicans saw Trump's win as permission to go on with conservative changes like deregulation, tax cuts, and a stronger national security strategy. With his win, the party's outsider and populist factions were acknowledged, departing from the conventional Republican wisdom.

Democratic Party:

Shock and Disappointment: The outcome first shocked and demoralized the Democratic Party. Many well-known Democrats who supported Clinton were shocked that their candidate had lost in spite of what seemed to be a clear advantage. The surprise setback forced the party to consider its options at a period of reckoning.

- Following the election, the Democratic Party received requests for reconsideration and introspection. The party's outreach initiatives, message, and strategy were questioned by leaders and activists. Well-known voices, including Hillary Clinton, stressed how important it was for the party to comprehend and respond to the concerns of the people who had voted for Trump.

- The Democratic Party already had splits, which the defeat brought to light. After endorsing Bernie Sanders in the primaries, progressive groups were irate with the party's establishment side. They said that the party's inability to engage working-class people and confront important problems like economic inequality was the cause of the defeat.

Public Analysts and the Media:

- Trump's win took the media by surprise. Numerous news outlets had projected that Clinton would win, and the evening turned out to be an exciting and disorganized occasion. Media outlets hurried to modify their reporting and provide an explanation for the outcome, with some analysts blaming Trump's victory on underappreciated demographic changes and the potency of his outsider campaign.

- There was a lot of polarization in the media's response. While some pundits emphasised the shortcomings of polling and forecasting models, others concentrated on the implications of Trump's victory for US democracy and foreign policy. The media's reaction turned into a source of conflict, with objections levelled at the precision of forecasts as well as the way the election results were presented.

International Community:

A combination of interest and uncertainty characterised the responses from throughout the world. Foreign nations and world leaders kept a careful eye on the election results because they knew how a Trump administration may affect world affairs. Both Trump's supporters and detractors were eager to ascertain how commerce, diplomacy, and foreign relations would be affected by his "America First" rhetoric. While some foreign dignitaries congratulated the new administration and pledged to collaborate with it, others expressed apprehension about possible changes to U.S. foreign policy. Discussions over trade agreements, international security, and transatlantic ties have been sparked by the election results.

People and Movements at the Grassroots:

- A wave of activity and demonstrations accompanied the grassroots reaction. The Women's March, which took place on January 21, 2017, came to symbolize the initial opposition to Trump's election. To voice their disapproval of Trump's actions and support progressive causes, activists and grassroots groups organised.

- A number of grassroots movements were sparked by the election, which raised resistance and involvement in politics. Many activists regarded Trump's win as a trigger for Organising efforts to fight his administration's policies and promote alternative agendas.

Business and Financial Sector

- The business and financial sectors saw substantial volatility after the election results. While there was early apprehension, markets quickly started to respond favourable to Trump's pledges of tax reform and deregulation. Investors and industry executives expected a business-friendly atmosphere under Trump's administration, leading to a rally in stock markets.

- Business executives started evaluating the potential effects of Trump's presidency on their sectors and areas of interest. The business sector undertook strategic planning and modifications in response to the expected changes in trade legislation, tax policy, and economic strategy.

Diverse first responses to Trump's electoral triumph were indicative of the larger political and social climate. A new period of political participation, conflict, and change was ushered in by the shock and exhilaration experienced by many groups. The answers provided context for the divisive and revolutionary years that followed by highlighting the profound differences in American politics and the international world.

CHAPTER NO. 02

THE TRUMP PRESIDENCY – FIRST TERM

"As Socrates once said, 'An unexamined life is not worth living.' The first term of the Trump presidency was a period of analysis and reawakening, challenging the status quo and striving to bring back the true essence of the American spirit."

There were major political, social, and economic changes during Donald J. Trump's first term as the 45th President of the United States, which ran from January 20, 2017, to January 20, 2021. His unique approach, contentious policies, and significant influence on both home and foreign affairs defined his administration.

2.1 Early Years and Major Conquests

With a rush of executive orders, Trump started his administration determined to carry out his campaign pledges. Two of his first accomplishments were the nomination of three justices to the Supreme Court—Neil Grouch, Brett Cavanaugh, and Amy Coney Barrett—which cemented a conservative majority on the court and the tax reform law that was completed in December 2017 and lowered corporate and individual tax rates. Deregulation was the central tenet of the Trump administration, which reversed many of the commercial and environmental rules enacted by earlier administrations. Among other things, Trump said that pulling out of the climate change accord in Paris would be bad for US economic interests.

Border and Immigration Policy

One of the main concerns of Trump's administration was immigration. He took a tough stand on immigration reform and border security, which was best shown by his divisive plan to build a wall between the United States and Mexico. Additionally, the Trump administration implemented a travel restriction that applies to a number of countries with a large Muslim population. This move sparked intense criticism and legal challenges. Families of migrants were split up at the southern border as a result of the administration's "zero-tolerance" policy, which generated strong opposition and discussions over immigration enforcement and human rights.

Trade and Foreign Policy

Trump's "America First" foreign policy prioritized American interests above those of other countries and reevaluated long-standing relationships and accords. In order to help American industry and workers, his government renegotiated NAFTA, resulting in the United States-Mexico-Canada Agreement (USMCA).

In addition, Trump adopted a combative approach towards China, imposing taxes on Chinese imports and starting a trade spat. The government was criticized for the economic effect of these tariffs, despite its attempts to resolve intellectual property concerns and trade imbalances. With several meetings between Trump and North Korean leader Kim Jong-un, the Trump administration's approach to North Korea was noticeably unorthodox. Though no official agreement was reached, the goal of these sessions was denuclearization.

Investigations and Impeachments

There was a great deal of political unrest throughout Trump's administration, including two impeachments. The House of Representatives impeached Trump in December 2019 on grounds of power abuse and obstruction of Congress pertaining to his dealings with the Ukrainian government. He was exonerated by the Senate in February 2020. After the Capitol riot on January 6, 2021, Trump was accused of inciting an uprising and faced a second impeachment attempt in January of the same year. Following his departure from office, Trump was exonerated at the Senate trial.

The COVID-19 pandemic

One of the most significant challenges of Trump's first term was the COVID-19 outbreak. In addition to major dispute over public health policies and communication techniques, the administration's reaction to the pandemic was characterised by quick vaccine development via Operation Warp Speed. Numerous facets of Trump's administration were impacted by the epidemic, including social unrest, economic downturns, and the final election result.

Political and Social Divides

Trump's administration widened already-existing political and socioeconomic divisions. Political and social tensions were raised as a result of his policies and statements, which often provoked divisive reactions. During his administration, demonstrations against police brutality, the Black Lives Matter movement, and racial relations all gained prominence. Trump's first term was marked by intense conflict and upheaval, which had a big impact on both US politics and international affairs. His administration changed a lot of U.S. policy and had a long-lasting effect on politics.

2.2   Major Policies and Achievements of the Trump Presidency

During his first year in office, Donald J. Trump accomplished a number of audacious and sometimes contentious goals and initiatives that sought to drastically alter the political and economic climate in the United States. The administration's aims and their effects on the home and foreign fronts are reflected in these significant policies and accomplishments.

2.2.1   Reforming Taxes

The Tax Cuts and Jobs Act (TCJA), which was passed in December 2017, was one of the main accomplishments of President Trump's tenure. This important piece of legislation reduced individual income tax rates temporarily and dropped the corporation tax rate from 35% to 21%. The intention was to boost consumer and company expenditure in order to promote economic development. The TCJA was criticized for increasing the federal deficit and largely benefitting wealthy persons and businesses, even if it was acknowledged that it had a short-term positive impact on the economy.

2.2.2 Deregulatory

The administration of Donald Trump made cutting federal regulations a top priority. The objective was to promote economic expansion and lessen the regulatory load on enterprises. The repeal of environmental restrictions like the Clean Power Plan and the Waters of the United States rule were two notable examples of deregulatory acts. In addition, the government changed or abolished a number of laws pertaining to healthcare, financial services, and workplace safety. Deregulation, according to supporters, increased economic activity while undermining consumer and environmental protections, according to detractors.

2.2.3 Medical Care

Regarding healthcare, Trump and the Republicans in Congress want to remove and replace the Affordable Care Act (ACA). Through the Tax Cuts and Jobs Act, the government was able to do away with the individual mandate penalty even if a complete repeal did not happen. In addition, the Trump administration reversed ACA rules and increased the number of short-term health insurance available. Although the goal of these modifications was to provide customers more flexibility and options, there was concern that they might weaken safeguards for those with pre-existing medical issues.

2.2.3 Immigration

Trump's immigration policies were a pillar of his administration. Important activities comprised:

- One of Trump's main campaign promises was to erect a wall separating the United States from Mexico. Although the wall was not finished under his administration, a significant chunk was built or strengthened.

- The Supreme Court subsequently affirmed an executive order that the administration had issued prohibiting travel from a number of countries with a large Muslim population. The government defended the restriction by citing it as an effort to improve national security.

- Due to the administration's implementation of a "zero-tolerance" policy for unauthorized border crossings, many family separations occurred. After receiving criticism, this policy was finally changed.

2.2.5 International Relations

Trump's "America First" foreign policy strategy was defined by:

- The United States-Mexico-Canada Agreement (USMCA) is the product of the administration's renegotiating of NAFTA. The USMCA sought to modernize trade regulations for the advantage of American industry and workers.

- In response to trade imbalances and intellectual property theft, Trump declared war on China by putting tariffs on Chinese imports. In addition to creating retaliatory tariffs and economic uncertainty, the tariffs were intended to coerce China into making trade concessions.

- Trump had direct discussions with Kim Jong-un, the leader of North Korea, which led to historic meetings. Although a formal agreement was not reached at the meetings, the goal was to denuclearize North Korea.

2.2.6 Reforming the Criminal Justice System

Trump enacted the First Step Act in December of 2018. This bipartisan criminal justice reform sought to enhance prison conditions, provide offenders greater opportunity for rehabilitation, and lower mandatory minimum terms for certain nonviolent crimes. The legislation received a lot of attention for tackling concerns with sentencing inequalities and mass imprisonment.

2.2.7 Environmental and Energy Policy

The development of fossil fuels and energy independence were pushed by the Trump administration. Among the major initiatives were the following:

- Trump issued executive orders to expedite the building of the contentious Keystone XL and Dakota Access Pipelines, which were deemed essential to the nation's energy infrastructure.
- The administration declared its plan to leave the climate change accord, claiming that it unfairly burdened the United States' economy and favored other nations.

2.2.8 Reaction to COVID-19

- Operation Warp Speed, a program to expedite the creation and dissemination of vaccinations, was a defining feature of the Trump administration's reaction to the COVID-19 pandemic. Although the administration's overall management of the epidemic attracted harsh criticism for its inconsistent message, difficulties with testing, and problems with public health coordination, the quick development of vaccinations was an important accomplishment.

Trump's bold moves and revolutionary initiatives to realign U.S. foreign and domestic policy helped to define his administration. The fact that there was a great deal of discussion and controversy around his administration's accomplishments shows how divisive American politics were at the time.

2.3   Economic Policies of the Trump Presidency

President Donald J. Trump pursued a number of economic initiatives during his first term with the goals of boosting GDP, overhauling the tax code, and lightening regulatory requirements. An outline of his main economic initiatives is provided below:

Tax Cuts and Jobs Act (TCJA)

One of Trump's most important legislative accomplishments was the Tax Cuts and Jobs Act, which was approved in December 2017. The TCJA sought to promote economic expansion by:

- In an effort to stimulate company investment and increase economic activity, the corporation tax rate was lowered from 35% to 21%.
- The Tax Cuts and Jobs Act (TCJA) temporarily reduced the rates of individual income taxes in a number of income categories until 2025.
- By providing a reduced one-time tax rate on these money, the act incentivized American corporations to repatriate their international profits.
- By making the filing process simpler, the standard deduction was almost doubled, which helped a lot of people.

- The Tax Cuts and Jobs Act eliminated the Affordable Care Act's individual mandate, which compelled people to have health insurance or pay a fine.
- The TCJA's proponents claimed that it boosted employment and economic expansion. Critics said that it failed to provide the anticipated long-term economic advantages and instead disproportionately favored rich people and companies, increasing the government debt.

Deregulatory

Trump's administration prioritized cutting down on federal regulations in order to promote economic expansion and get rid of what was seen to be onerous government oversight:

- The government repealed a number of laws pertaining to financial services, healthcare, and environmental protection, among other industries. The Waters of the United States rule, which increased federal jurisdiction over wetlands and streams, and the Clean Power Plan, which sought to reduce carbon emissions from power plants, were two notable rollbacks.
- The "two-for-one" executive order mandated that federal agencies remove two regulations for each new one they introduce. The overarching goal of this approach was to lessen the regulatory load.

Influence and Disagreement: Deregulation proponents claimed that more corporate investment and economic expansion resulted from it. Opponents, however, voiced worries about possible harm to the environment, public safety, and health.

Tariffs and Trade Policy

A turn towards protectionism and a focus on renegotiating trade agreements were hallmarks of Trump's trade strategy:

- The North American Free Trade Agreement (NAFTA) was superseded by the United States, Mexico, and Canada Agreement (USMCA). By enhancing labour standards, expanding access to the agricultural market, and encouraging more equitable trade practices, the pact aims to help American workers.
- In response to trade imbalances and intellectual property theft, Trump declared war on China by putting taxes on billions of dollars' worth of Chinese products. China responded with tariffs of its own, sparking a protracted trade spat.
- Citing national security concerns, the government slapped tariffs on imports of steel and aluminum under Section 232 of the Trade Expansion Act. These tariffs impacted international commerce and strained ties with important partners.
- The goals of Trump's trade policy were to balance trade imbalances and safeguard American businesses. They were required, according to its supporters, to counter unfair commercial practices. However, opponents cautioned that tariffs may hurt US companies and consumers by raising prices and upsetting supply networks.

Employment and Infrastructure

Despite being a major campaign pledge, there wasn't much legislative progress made in the area of infrastructure. The government did, however, take the following actions in regards to infrastructure and employment creation:

- In order to upgrade public transportation, bridges, and highways, Trump put out a $1.5 trillion infrastructure proposal. The idea, which encountered opposition in Congress and failed to produce full law, aimed to use public funds as a means of attracting private investment.

- The government made a point of generating jobs via a number of programs, such as measures to lessen the regulatory load on companies and programs for vocational training.

- Impact and Controversy: Despite some improvements in job creation and infrastructure projects, legislative deadlock and conflicting agendas made the administration's objectives in these areas difficult to achieve.

Policy on Energy

The growth of fossil fuel output and energy independence were prioritized in Trump's energy policy:

- The administration took back a number of laws, including the Clean Power Plan that were designed to lower carbon emissions. Promoting the development and use of fossil fuels, such as coal, oil, and natural gas, was the aim.

- In order to move natural gas and oil across North America, Trump backed the building of important energy infrastructure projects including the Dakota Access and Keystone XL pipelines.

- The goal of Trump's energy policy was to promote domestic energy companies and increase American energy independence. Critics voiced worries about the effects on the environment and the sustainability of relying too much on fossil fuels in the long run.

Trump's economic agenda included large tax cuts, trade protectionist measures, deregulation, and an emphasis on energy independence.

The goals of these programs were to improve the US economy in a number of areas and encourage economic development. Even if they partially succeeded in their objectives, they also generated a great deal of discussion and controversy, which highlighted how difficult and often divisive his administration's economic policies was.

2.4   Foreign Relations of the Trump Presidency

In his approach to international affairs, President Donald J. Trump combined strong nationalism, trade deal renegotiation, and nontraditional diplomacy. During his administration, the United States' foreign policy saw substantial changes that were typified by a departure from custom and an emphasis on putting American interests first.

The America First Doctrine

Trump's "America First" foreign policy stance, which placed a premium on American interests above those of other countries, served as the cornerstone of his foreign policy strategy. This strategy was seen in numerous significant changes to policy:

- Despite the potential for strained ties with long-standing partners, Trump often sought unilateral moves that he felt would immediately benefit the United States. This included reviewing long-standing ties and pulling out of international accords.
- Trump's "America First" strategy included a major emphasis on balancing trade ties and cutting trade deficits. In order to better serve American economic interests, he attempted to renegotiate trade accords.

Economic and Trade Relations

The Trump administration took a combative approach to trade, especially with important trading partners:

- Imposing tariffs on Chinese imports valued at hundreds of billions of dollars, the Trump administration started a trade war with China. The government sought to resolve trade imbalances, unfair trade practices, and theft of intellectual property. Global supply networks were interrupted by the crisis, which also resulted in retaliatory tariffs from China.
- The USMCA, or United States-Mexico-Canada Agreement, was aimed at modernizing economic ties with Canada and Mexico after Trump renegotiated NAFTA. The pact sought to increase market access for American products and services and improve labour standards for the benefit of American workers.
- Trump also criticized trade policies with the EU, emphasizing the need to repair trade imbalances and reduce trade deficits. He fought for more equitable trade deals and threatened to impose taxes on products coming from Europe.

Connections with Important Partners and Allies

Trump's foreign policy strategy significantly altered US ties with both long-standing allies and international partners:

- Trump put pressure on partners to boost their payments after criticizing them for failing to fulfil their defence budget obligations. Despite the fact that this approach was meant to promote burden-sharing, it caused conflict with friends in Europe.

- The Trump administration made a number of significant moves in the region, including:

- The U.S. Embassy was moved from Tel Aviv to Jerusalem after Trump formally recognized Jerusalem as the capital of Israel. Leaders in Palestine and other foreign entities criticized this contentious action.

- Mediated by the government, these agreements restored diplomatic ties between Israel and a number of Arab countries, notably Bahrain and the United Arab Emirates. In the area, this was considered a major diplomatic win.

- The Joint Comprehensive Plan of Action (JCPOA), sometimes referred to as the Iran nuclear agreement, was withdrawn by President Trump. He reinstated the sanctions on Iran, citing worries about its regional policies and nuclear program.

- Trump and Russia's connection came under close analysis. Even while Trump said that he wanted to see better ties with Moscow, his administration sanctioned the country for a number of offences, including as meddling in elections and aggression in Ukraine.

The Korean Peninsula

Trump's strategy against North Korea was typified by meetings with great visibility and direct diplomacy:

- Trump had direct discussions with Kim Jong-un, the leader of North Korea, making history as the first sitting US president to do so. The goal of the summits was to strengthen bilateral ties while addressing North Korea's nuclear weapons development.

- Not much progress was achieved in the denuclearization discussions, even with the high-profile sessions. In order to confront North Korea's nuclear aspirations, the Trump administration pursued diplomatic avenues while maintaining a firm position on sanctions.

International Accords and Coalitions

Under President Trump, a number of multilateral accords and coalitions were reassessed:

- Citing concerns about the agreement's conditions' perceived injustice and the economic effect on American industry, Trump withdrew the United States from the climate change accord.
- A global trade pact including numerous Pacific Rim nations, Trump withdrew from the TPP.
- He said that the pact was bad for American companies and workers.
- Trump has often questioned the efficacy of the UN and criticized it. In addition to criticizing several UN decisions and programs, he attempted to lower US payments to the organisation.

Foreign and Humanitarian Aid

The Trump administration revised American foreign assistance programs:

- Stressing a focus on home priorities and a more transactional approach to global assistance, the administration recommended major cutbacks to foreign aid programs.
- The administration often combined diplomatic pressure with targeted humanitarian help when responding to different humanitarian crises, such as the civil war in Syria and the situation in Venezuela.

The "America First" tenet of President Trump shaped his approach to international affairs and resulted in substantial changes to American foreign policy. Confrontational trade policies, direct diplomacy with important countries, and a reassessment of international accords and alliances were all part of his administration's strategy. A great deal of discussion and influence on international relations resulted from these policies, even if some of them were intended to further American interests and accomplish certain objectives.

2.5   Security at borders and immigration

Immigration and border security were major concerns during Donald Trump's administration, influencing a large portion of his domestic policy agenda. His administration's strategy was characterised by a number of assertive laws and programs meant to combat illegal immigration, fortify the southern border of the United States, and reform the country's immigration laws.

Building of Border Walls

The construction of a wall along the border between the United States and Mexico was one of Trump's most notable campaign pledges. The government worked very hard to fulfil this promise: Trump asked Congress for a large amount of money to construct the wall, but he encountered opposition and difficulties getting the money in full. In spite of this, his government was able to set aside funds for the building of new barriers and the renovation of border infrastructure. Several hundred miles of new fence and obstacles had been constructed or rebuilt by the time of his term's conclusion. To speed up wall building and strengthen border security, Trump signed executive orders. In order to speed up environmental and regulatory evaluations and enable wall building, these directives contained exemptions.

The Zero-Tolerance Policy and Divorce

The contentious "zero-tolerance" policy, which was put into effect by the government to discourage illegal immigration,

- All those who entered the country illegally, including those who were applying for asylum, were to be prosecuted under the zero-tolerance policy. Families were forced to split up as a result, with kids being held in juvenile facilities and their parents being prosecuted.
- Lawmakers, the public, and human rights groups all strongly opposed the program. Even when the government changed course in June 2018, the effects of family separations sparked debate and legal challenges.

Deportations and Immigration Enforcement

The Trump administration stepped up attempts to boost deportations and enforce immigration laws:

- The administration gave U.S. Immigration and Customs Enforcement (ICE) more authority to carry out raids and remove unknown individuals. This includes focusing on those who had overstayed their visas and had a history of criminal convictions.
- The Trump administration aimed to impose stricter measures on these localities, which restrict their cooperation with federal immigration officials. The goal of the executive directives and proposed laws was to enhance enforcement actions and withdraw federal funding from certain communities.

Travel Prohibitions and Refugee Acceptance

Trump enacted a number of policies that have an impact on refugee admittance and immigration from certain nations:

- The administration imposed a number of travel restrictions on nations with a mostly Muslim population. Despite facing legal challenges, the Supreme Court ultimately sustained the prohibitions in a modified version. Preventing immigration from nations considered to be a threat to national security was the goal of the restrictions.
- The government drastically cut the amount of refugees who were permitted to resettle in the US. The necessity to put domestic security above refugee resettlement and worries about national security were the main drivers of this drop.

Lawful Visa and Immigration Regulations

The legal immigration and visa procedures were also affected by Trump's policies:

- The administration aimed to modify the H-1B visa scheme, which permits proficient foreign laborers to get employment authorization in the United States. Increasing the inspection of visa applications and advocating for laws that give preference to American workers were among the changes.
- If immigrants were thought to be likely to depend on public assistance, the administration imposed a new "public charge" regulation that would make it more difficult for them to get green cards. The goal of this regulation was to guarantee that immigrants could sustain themselves financially without needing help from the government.

Legislation and Immigration Reform

Aims were made during Trump's presidency to change the larger immigration system:

- To address concerns about border security, legal immigration, and the status of undocumented immigrants, the administration suggested a number of immigration reform proposals. Nevertheless, there was a lot of resistance to these ideas, and they mostly failed to pass Congress.
- A divisive topic, the Deferred Action for Childhood Arrivals (DACA) program offered protections to illegal immigrants brought to the country as minors. Due to Trump's attempts to terminate the program, there were legal disputes and a brief extension of DACA protections while the Supreme Court made judgements.

Trump's domestic policy program was heavily focused on immigration and border security, with bold efforts to strengthen border security, reduce illegal immigration, and reform the immigration system. Significant discussion and controversy were generated by his administration's policies, which included building the border wall, adopting a zero-tolerance stance, and altering the visa and refugee procedures. Discussions in the US over immigration and border security are still influenced by these measures.

2.6   Challenges and Opposition

Donald Trump's administration encountered several obstacles and resistance throughout his first term, which had a big influence on how his policies were carried out and received.

Opposition to politics

- Democrats, who often disagreed with Trump's policy recommendations, were a constant obstacle for the president. This was seen in a number of important domains, such as budget discussions, healthcare, and immigration. Government shutdowns and standoffs were common as a result of congressional resistance, especially when it came to matters like financing for border walls.

- During his first term, the House of Representatives twice attempted to remove President Trump from office. The first impeachment, which occurred in December 2019, was linked to claims of power abuse and obstruction of Congress about his interactions with the Ukrainian government. Following the Capitol riot on January 6, 2021, Trump was accused of inciting an uprising in the second impeachment. Both of the impeachments posed serious obstacles to his administration and exposed the stark political divide in the United States.

Legal Obstacles

- The courts heard objections to a number of Trump's measures. For instance, he was sued many times for his travel restrictions and efforts to terminate DACA. Courts often intervened to halt or alter his executive orders and programs, typically bringing up procedural flaws, constitutional rights, or previous legal cases.

- The Supreme Court examined a number of Trump administration policies, such as the travel restrictions and the "public charge" regulation. There has been continuous judicial analysis and opposition to the administration's initiatives, resulting in the limiting or overturning of some measures while maintaining others in modified versions.

Public Perception and Media Criticism

- Trump and the media had a contentious relationship that was evident on a regular basis. The media landscape became divisive and acrimonious as a result of his frequent attacks on journalists and criticism of major media sites as "fake news." This antagonistic connection shaped public opinion and contributed to the divisiveness of political debate.

- Trump's policies, especially those concerning immigration and healthcare, have caused large-scale demonstrations and reactions from the general population. For instance, the zero-tolerance policy's effect on family separations sparked large-scale public uproar and demonstrations, which had an impact on the administration's reputation and the way its policies were carried out.

Internal Management Difficulties

- There was a lot of staff turnover in Trump's administration, with some important posts being repeatedly filled by interim officials or replaced. This volatility exacerbated internal problems and disruptions while impairing the efficacy and continuity of policy execution.

- There were administrative and logistical obstacles in the way of putting certain policies into action, including building the border wall. The obstacles faced in obtaining funds, managing environmental laws, and collaborating with state and local government agencies affected the speed and extent of policy implementation.

- Trade Wars: Trade wars impacted international economic relations as a result of Trump's trade policies, which included tariffs on China and other trading partners. Retaliatory tariffs and a disruption in international commerce as a consequence of these trade conflicts affected American consumers and companies.

- Trump's foreign policy strategy has hurt ties with enduring friends due to his criticism of NATO and conventional allies. His "America First" stance often caused rifts with other nations and made it difficult to maintain international alliances.

Health Crisis and Pandemic Response

The Trump administration faced an unprecedented difficulty as a result of the COVID-19 pandemic. The management of testing, public health recommendations, and communication throughout the pandemic response drew criticism. The administration's pandemic strategy, which included messaging and collaboration with state governments, came under criticism and sparked discussion in the public and political spheres.

Cultural and Social Concerns

Racial and social tensions increased throughout Trump's administration, especially after the Charlottesville rally and the Black Lives Matter demonstrations. His opinions on these matters were often divisive and influenced national discussions about inequality, justice, and race. Significant obstacles and resistance from the political, legal, media, and public domains characterised Trump's administration. During his first term, these difficulties affected the administration's capacity to carry out programs and molded the larger political environment. His controversial administration, together with other domestic and global challenges, made for a complicated and often polarizing time in American politics.

2.7   Media and Political Opposition

The government of Donald Trump encountered severe criticism and scrutiny from political rivals and the media throughout his first term in office, which had a big influence on the political environment and the efficacy of his presidency.

Opposition in the Media

- Trump received a lot of negative publicity from the mainstream media. News organisations routinely brought attention to scandals, policy errors, and individual scandals, which exacerbated the already divisive media landscape. Trump's divisive rhetoric—which included criticism of the media—only made matters worse. His designation of prominent news outlets as "enemies of the people" and "fake news" strained ties even further and increased public mistrust of media narratives.

- Under Trump's administration, a lot of investigative journalism was produced on subjects including the Mueller probe that followed and the suspected Russian meddling in the 2016 election. Public discussions regarding the administration's actions were sparked by media reports on these probes, as well as information on other purported conflicts of interest and legal matters.

- One of the main aspects of Trump's administration has been his use of social media, especially Twitter. Through Twitter, he often engaged the people directly and circumvented regular media outlets. But this open contact also brought to a lot of disputes and arguments with the media. Public debate was greatly influenced by social media platforms, and Trump's social media presence often served as a focal point for both criticism and praise.

Opposition in Politics

- The Democratic majority in the House of Representatives was one of the main sources of resistance to Trump's administration. Proposals for significant legislation, such as those pertaining to immigration, healthcare, and tax reform, encountered opposition and heated discussion. Government shutdowns and challenges in accomplishing the administration's legislative agenda were often caused by the party divide and the regular deadlocks.

- There were two impeachment procedures during Trump's administration. The first impeachment attempt, which began in December 2019, was based on claims that Trump had misused his authority by asking Ukraine to look into a political opponent and interfering with Congress's impeachment investigation. Following the Capitol riot on January 6, 2021, Trump was accused of inciting an uprising in the second impeachment. The fierce political opposition and divides that marked his reign culminated in these hearings.

- State and local governments opposed certain of Trump's proposals, especially those pertaining to immigration and public health. For instance, a lot of state officials opposed his immigration proposals, which included limits on sanctuary cities and building a wall along the border. Similar disagreements over lockdown protocols and public health recommendations arose with state governors during his management of the COVID-19 epidemic.

- The Republican Party presented difficulties for Trump's leadership. Republicans were divided throughout his administration, with several publicly criticizing his attitude or ideas. The intricacies of his relationship with the larger GOP establishment were reflected in the many legislative votes and public remarks that revealed this internal discord.

- State and federal courts presented the Trump administration with a number of legal obstacles. Legal challenges to policies like travel bans and the effort to terminate the Deferred Action for Childhood Arrivals (DACA) program sometimes led to court blockades or adjustments. The administration's attempts to carry out its program were met with more resistance as a result of these judicial challenges.

During Trump's first term, the media and political opposition were vital in determining the course of the administration and the public's opinion. The tense relationship with the media, together with strong political opposition and legal difficulties, produced a complicated and often divisive atmosphere. This resistance affected not only how successful Trump's programs were but also contributed to the larger arguments and rifts that marked his presidency.

2.8   Public Perception and Grassroots Support

Although the public's assessment of Donald Trump's administration was much divided, he nonetheless had a sizable and ardent base of grassroots support. Gaining knowledge of these relationships helps one to comprehend the wider effects of his administration on American culture.

Public View

- The public's perspectives were sharply split throughout Trump's administration. Trump was seen by his followers as a revolutionary leader who stood up to the political elite and championed the needs of regular Americans. His unorthodox methods and direct connection struck a chord with those who were fed up with conventional politics. On the other hand, a lot of his detractors saw him as a divisive character whose words and actions threatened democratic institutions and standards.

- Public opinion was greatly influenced by how the media portrayed certain topics. The highlighting of scandals and controversies by mainstream media outlets contributed to a poor perception among readers of conventional news sources. On the other hand, Trump's own social media channels and alternative media outlets offered a story that resonated with his supporters, portraying him as a hero fighting an unfair system.

- Throughout his presidency, Trump's approval ratings saw considerable swings. There were times when his popularity surged, especially after significant policy victories or protests, but there were also times when it fell precipitously in the wake of scandals like how the COVID-19 epidemic was handled when the impeachment process began. These swings were a reflection of how deeply ingrained and divisive his public persona was.

Community-Based Assistance

- A key component of Trump's grassroots backing was the "Make America Great Again" (MAGA) movement. Restoring American greatness, opposing political correctness, and tackling problems like immigration and trade were the movement's main points of convergence. MAGA fans were very active, planning events and demonstrations as well as encouraging people to vote via social media and neighbourhood gatherings.

- A defining feature of Trump's administration and a vital part of his base of support were his rallies. Enthusiastic audiences were a defining feature of these events, which often provided Trump with a direct line to his supporters. Supporters were able to voice their opinions and fortify their feeling of belonging and common goal throughout the rallies.

- Trump's use of social media played a crucial role in establishing and maintaining support from the general public. He was able to communicate directly with his fans and avoid conventional media by using social media sites like Facebook and Twitter. His words spread more easily as a result of their direct contact, which also inspired grassroots activists. Social media groups and forums among other online communities were crucial in coordinating support and spreading data in accordance with Trump's goals.

- The emergence of pro-Trump organisations and local action were further indications of the grassroots movement. Local branches of conservative organisations, including the Tea Party and several pro-Trump PACs, strove to further his agenda and bolster his chances of winning reelection. These groups engaged in a wide range of activities, including voter registration campaigns and grassroots lobbying.

- A large portion of Trump's base saw his election as a direct reaction to social and economic injustices. Working-class voters who felt left behind by the economic shifts of the preceding decades were drawn to the promise of economic revival via tax cuts, deregulation, and job creation. Furthermore, his constituency was very responsive to social concerns like immigration reform and conservative court nominations.

Obstacles to Community Support

- Despite the fact that Trump had strong support from the grassroots, there were some difficulties. Disagreements over strategy and policy sometimes resulted from internal splits within the GOP and among his supporters. Trump's own language and strategy, which may annoy moderate supporters or cause conflict with more conventional Republican voters, sometimes made these splits worse.

- There was a lot of opposition to Trump's administration from a variety of sources, such as coordinated rallies, demonstrations, and political involvement from opposing forces. This opposition often emphasised how divisive his administration was and how difficult it is to retain unwavering popular support in the face of intense scandal.

Despite having a much divided public image going into his administration, Trump had a strong and organised network of grassroots supporters. This support was maintained and mobilized in large part by the MAGA movement, demonstrations, social media interaction, and local involvement. Trump's capacity to energies his supporters and influence public opinion, in spite of obstacles and disagreements, highlights the important role that grassroots movements play in modern American politics.

2.9   Rallying the "forgotten man and woman"

Donald Trump's appeal to the "forgotten man and woman"—a wide category that includes supporters who felt disregarded and alienated by the political establishment—was one of the main themes of his administration. This constituency had a pivotal role in molding his political persona and tactics, impacting not just his discourse but also his agenda items.

Tracking Down the "Forgotten Man and Woman"

- A large portion of Trump's base was made up of working-class or rural residents who had lost their jobs as a result of deindustrialization, Globalisation, and technological advancement. These people often felt left behind by political figures, whom they saw as being more preoccupied with the interests of the metropolitan elite.

- These voters also expressed a feeling of cultural and social estrangement in addition to economic worries. They saw an increasing dissonance between their beliefs and the dominant cultural narratives propagated by educational establishments and the mass media. Their sensation of being ignored was mostly influenced by factors like immigration, traditional values, and national identity.

- Members of the "forgotten" group often voiced their displeasure with what they saw to be an ineffective and corrupt political system. They believed that their opinions were not being heard in the corridors of power and that the promises made by politicians were not being kept. Perceptions of the incompetence and corruption of the administration added to this disappointment.

Trump's Strategy and Messaging

- A clear appeal to those fed up with entrenched political elites, Trump's slogan "Drain the Swamp" As an outsider with no connections to the Washington elite, Trump made the pledge to rid the government of the corruption and inefficiencies that many believed were a problem.

- The working class's financial complaints were intended to be addressed by Trump's economic initiatives, which include tax cuts, deregulation, and trade changes. In order to boost sectors and provide chances for his supporters, Trump made promises to renegotiate trade agreements, bring jobs back to America, and lessen the burden of regulations on companies.

- Trump's speech often touched on issues that his supporters found relevant to their social and cultural problems. Many members of his base agreed with his emphasis on topics like immigration restriction, the defence of Second Amendment rights, and hostility to political correctness. He successfully rallied support and strengthened his bond with the "forgotten" people by addressing these concerns.

- Trump's appeal to these people was greatly aided by his use of social media. He was able to deliver his views, answer criticism, and mobilize support in a manner that seemed more direct and immediate to his followers by eschewing conventional media and speaking with his audience directly on social media sites like Twitter.

The Effects of Gathering "Forgotten Man and Woman"

- In crucial swing states during the 2016 election, the tactic of appealing to the "forgotten man and woman" was effective. Through his emphasis on topics that these people found most important and his portrayal of himself as an advocate for their needs, Trump was able to win significant wins in areas like Pennsylvania, Michigan, and Wisconsin.

- A wider realignment in American politics was facilitated by Trump's ability to mobilize this group. It brought attention to the growing significance of rural and working-class voters in the political sphere, causing both main parties to concentrate on resolving their problems and concerns.

- Trump's policies and language were shaped by the focus on the "forgotten man and woman" throughout his administration. It continued to be a major issue in his political speeches and an important part of his 2020 campaign platform. This emphasis strengthened his identification as an advocate for those who felt left out of the political system and helped him stay in touch with his base.

Obstacles and Remarks

- Although Trump's plea to the "forgotten man and woman" struck a chord with many, it was not without criticism. His strategy was criticized by some as being exclusive, claiming that it ignored other significant topics and people. His initiatives, according to his detractors, sometimes unduly rewarded the rich or neglected to address underlying disparities.
- Trump's administration came under fire for inconsistencies in his statements and deeds. For instance, certain of his measures, such tax cuts for the rich, were seen as at odds with his message of economic revitalization for the ordinary American, even if he had promised to promote the working class.

The "forgotten man and woman" rallying was a key component of Donald Trump's presidential campaign strategy. Through concentrating on the political, cultural, and economic complaints of this group, Trump was able to assemble a devoted and robust following. His strategy changed the political environment by emphasizing how crucial it is to address the issues raised by those who felt marginalized by the establishment. His approach was contentious and powerful, but it also highlighted the long-standing grievances and hopes of a large segment of the American voter.

2.10   The rise of the "Make America Great Again" movement

Beginnings and Development

- During his 2016 presidential campaign, Donald Trump popularized the slogan "Make America Great Again" (MAGA). Trump repackaged and revitalized the term as the main rallying cry for his campaign, even though Ronald Reagan had previously used a similar phrase in his 1980 presidential campaign. The catchphrase struck a deep chord with a portion of the American public by capturing a wide feeling of nostalgia and a longing for a return to imagined previous glory.

- MAGA capitalized on the general dissatisfaction with the status of the country. The campaign slogan promised a return to a more affluent and well-respected America, since many Americans believed the nation had drifted from its core ideals. It conjured up feelings of lost American exceptionalism and the hope that the country might rise again with clear action and strong leadership.

Messaging and Campaign Strategy

- An emphasis on economic nationalism was fundamental to the MAGA movement. During his campaign, Trump pledged to rework trade agreements, impose taxes on imports, and boost local manufacturing in order to revive American industry. Working-class voters who believed that prior trade policies had resulted in job losses and economic stagnation were the target audience for this economic approach.

- The populist language of the MAGA movement positioned Trump as an outsider taking on the political establishment. The catchphrase became into a symbol of defiance against the establishment, which Trump described as dishonest and incompetent. Trump garnered support from individuals who felt left out of the political and economic system by portraying his campaign as a conflict between the powerful and the people.

- Drawing on worries about immigration, law and order, and traditional values, the MAGA movement also concentrated on these themes. Trump's campaign pledged to solve these concerns, which were seen to have been compromised by the actions of past administrations, in order to bolster national identity and restore pride in the country.

The phenomena of the MAGA Rally

- The MAGA movement grew to be associated with Trump's rallies. These grandiose gatherings provided his followers with a stage on which to deliver his teachings. The rallies' vibrant environment and passionate attendance served to further emphasise the attendees' feeling of camaraderie and common goal.

- During these events, Trump spoke with his supporters face-to-face and often addressed their issues and complaints. Additionally, Trump was able to avoid conventional media outlets—which he often attacked for their unfavourable coverage—by using the rallies. Trump was able to successfully mobilize support and reaffirm his themes by speaking with his supporters personally.

Influence on the Political Environment

- A major factor in Trump's election victory was the MAGA movement. A sizable segment of the American voters connected with the phrase and the policies it was linked to, especially in crucial swing states. Trump won victory in states crucial to his presidential ascent because of the movement's focus on national pride and economic recovery.

- A more general realignment in American politics was facilitated by the ascent of MAGA. The movement brought attention to the growing significance of nationalist and populist views, causing both main parties to concentrate on working-class and rural voters' issues. The political landscape was changed by this realignment, which also had an impact on the platforms and tactics of later election campaigns.

- The MAGA movement had an impact that went beyond the results of the 2016 election. It shaped Trump's leadership even further and served as a major campaign subject for his 2020 reelection. A significant section of the electorate continues to find resonance in many of the movement's ideas and beliefs, which have had a long-lasting effect on American politics.

Disagreements and Arguments

- The MAGA movement's detractors said that its speech often encouraged conflict and division. Some people believed that the emphasis on nationalism and populism exacerbated social and political divides, especially when it came to matters of race, immigration, and cultural values.

- A number of the MAGA movement's objectives, like trade tariffs and immigration restrictions, have come under fire for their drawbacks. These initiatives, according to their detractors, might worsen consumer prices, damage international relations, and raise economic instability.

A major change in American politics was signalled by the emergence of the "Make America Great Again" campaign. The movement connected with a large portion of the voters by fusing economic nationalism, populist rhetoric, and cultural issues. It was crucial to Donald Trump's electoral success. Beyond the results of the 2016 election, its influence shaped both main parties' strategy and later political debate. Even while the movement saw significant progress, it was not without controversy and criticism, which is indicative of the complicated and sometimes polarising character of modern American politics.

Chapter No. 03
The Deep State and Media Deception

The phrase "Deep State" describes a clandestine network of powerful people and organisations within a government that function without the consent of elected authorities or the general public. It is said that this covert network has considerable power and influence on political and policy choices, often going against the democratic process and the electorate's wishes.

Historical Origins and Interpretation

The Deep State idea is not brand-new. Historically, covert power networks inside different administrations have been described using similar concepts. The phrase initially described a covert coalition of bureaucratic and military elites influencing politics in secret in Turkey. The idea has developed in the United States to refer to a well-established political and bureaucratic elite that is seen to have undue influence on government.

Important Elements

- **Unelected Bureaucracy:** The core of Deep State accusations is the idea that unelected personnel in law enforcement and intelligence services have unchecked power to affect political and policy decisions without being held accountable to the public. Opponents contend that these organisations sometimes pursue their own goals while acting independently of elected politicians.

- **Political and Economic Interests:** The Deep State is often linked to influential political and business elites who are seen to put their own interests ahead of the interests of the broader public. This includes powerful businesspeople, lobbyists, and well-established political personalities who have the ability to influence or control policy choices in order to further their own objectives.
- **Covert Operations:** The Deep State is distinguished by its covert undertakings. This covers clandestine activities, insider information, and backroom Maneuvring with the intention of influencing political results. It is claimed that these covert activities control or affect public policy and governance outside of the democratic process.

Disputations and Accusations

- **Election Interference:** The Deep State theory's proponents assert that this network attempts to rig or meddle in elections. To accomplish desired political outcomes, there are allegations of efforts to disparage politicians, manipulate voter opinion, or even tamper with election results.
- **Political Persecution:** It is said that the Deep State uses smear campaigns, legal proceedings, and investigations to pursue political opponents. It is said that these acts are intended to discredit or undercut those who disagree with the status quo or the goals of powerful elites.

- **Control of Information:** It's also thought that the Deep State controls information to sway public opinion. To preserve power and influence, this involves influencing media coverage, stifling opposing viewpoints, and spreading false information.

3.1   The Deep State and Donald Trump

With the election of Donald Trump, the Deep State theory gained widespread acceptance. Trump and his allies have often claimed that the Deep State is working against him in his government. They cited investigations as proof of secret attempts to undermine his administration, like as the Mueller inquiry into suspected Russian meddling in the 2016 election. In reaction, Trump reorganized important roles inside the federal bureaucracy and attacked agencies openly those he felt were working against him.

3.2   Public Perception and Impact

Some sections of the public have found resonance with the concept of the Deep State, especially those who have lost faith in government agencies. Political polarization has resulted from it; some see it as a legitimate worry about unbridled power and corruption, while others write it off as a hoax. Discussions about accountability, transparency, and the impact of strong elites on democratic processes have been triggered by this idea. A variety of claims about covert power and influence networks throughout governments are included in the Deep State idea. Its enduring worries about accountability and the integrity of democratic institutions are reflected in its historical origins, salient characteristics, and contentious issues. These concepts still have an influence on popular views of government and political discourse.

3.3　Alleged Activities and Influence of the Deep State

Proponents of the Deep State theory contend that a variety of purported actions and spheres of influence erode democratic processes and public confidence. It is said that in order to accomplish certain goals, these operations include political scheming, information manipulation, and covert operations. An outline of the main domains where the Deep State is thought to have an impact is provided below:

3.3.1　Election Interference

- The Deep State is charged with influencing public opinion about political topics and candidates via the media and other information channels. This involves disseminating false or misleading information to undermine opponents or sway voters' decisions.
- There have been accusations that the Deep State participates in clandestine operations to rig elections in order to support firmly held political beliefs. These operations include interfering with voting machines and altering voter records.

3.3.2　Manipulation of Law and Politics

- Prominent enquiries like the Mueller probe into Russian meddling in the 2016 presidential election are often used as examples of Deep State actions intended to weaken public officials. Opponents claim that these enquiries are used to intimidate or discredit political rivals.

- It is said that the Deep State use legal means to single out and obstruct political opponents. This involves planning legal challenges, carrying out investigations with political motivations, or intimidating people using the legal system.

3.3.3   Intelligence gathering and covert operations

- It is thought that the Deep State conducts widespread monitoring and intelligence-gathering activities, sometimes without the public's knowledge or approval. This involves keeping an eye on activists, public leaders, and regular people in order to keep things under control and quell criticism.

- There have been allegations of the establishment of covert alliances between intelligence services, government officials, and influential commercial interests. It is believed that these coalitions collaborate behind the scenes to influence political and policy choices.

3.3.4   Media and Information Control

- It is said that the Deep State manipulates media coverage in order to sway public perception and narratives. This may be putting pressure on media organisations, influencing editorial choices, or fabricating articles to support certain agendas in the eyes of the general public.

- It is said that the Deep State suppresses material that contradicts the mainstream narrative and censors dissident voices. This involves smearing or suppressing journalists, activists, or whistleblowers who reveal uncomfortable facts.

3.3.5 Political and Economic Preference

- The Deep State is often associated with strong corporate interests that have a say in how politics are decided. This involves gaining government contracts, influencing political results via the use of economic power, and lobbying for the adoption of beneficial legislation.
- It is said that the Deep State influences policy choices in order to favor certain businesses or factions. This may include formulating rules, passing laws, or offering assistance from the government to groups that serve the interests of the privileged.

3.3.6 Undermining Institutions of Democracy

- It is thought that the Deep State impedes efforts and changes put forward by elected authorities by using bureaucratic opposition and lethargy. This entails keeping things as they are, obstructing the implementation of new policies, and postponing or blocking policy changes.
- There have been allegations that the Deep State subverts democracy via its actions. This involves efforts to undermine democratic institutions, rig elections, and reduce the power of elected officials.

3.4 Public Perception and Debate

There is a lot of disagreement on the existence and impact of the so-called "Deep State." Advocates contend that these purported actions expose a covert power structure that threatens democratic government. On the other hand, detractors see the Deep State as an exaggerated conspiracy theory that simplifies intricate political and institutional relationships. The current discussion is a reflection of larger worries about accountability, transparency, and the distribution of power in democracies. There are many powerful and clandestine actions that the Deep State is said to be involved in, such as media control, political manipulation, electoral meddling, clandestine operations, and economic favoritism. These assertions are a reflection of long-standing worries over the fairness of democratic procedures and the impact of covert power structures.

3.5   Media's Role in Politics

The storyline of political events, public opinion, and political landscapes are all significantly shaped by the media. Depending on the political environment and media practices, this impact may be both good and detrimental. This is a summary of the main points and ramifications of the media's relationship with politics:

3.5.1   Creating Public Opinion

- The media may shape public opinion by presenting political topics in ways that the general public finds appealing and understands. This entails deciding which tales to emphasise, arranging them, and using language that shapes the story as a whole. For instance, portraying an economic slump as the outcome of certain policies might influence the public's perception of those policies and those who support them.
- The media shapes the political agenda by deciding which subjects to cover and how much emphasis to place on them. This may influence which topics are marginalized and which gain prominence in public conversation. The public discourse and political agenda may be shaped by the media's emphasis on certain problems.

3.5.2 Information and Accountability Provision

- By looking into and documenting instances of political corruption, wrongdoing, and power abuses, the media acts as a watchdog. Investigative journalism has the power to reveal injustice and hold elected officials responsible, upholding democratic values and openness.

- It is the duty of media organisations to confirm facts and provide correct information. In order to combat false information and guarantee that the public has access to trustworthy information while making political choices, effective fact-checking is necessary.

3.5.3 Affecting Political Campaigns and Elections

- Election results may be greatly influenced by media coverage of political campaigns and politicians. Voters' opinions and choices might be influenced by favourable or unfavourable media. Candidates may gain credibility and influence public opinion by receiving endorsements from reputable media sources or prominent journalists.

- To spread ads, connect with voters, and advance their messages, political campaigns make use of media outlets. Media advertising has the power to mobilize supporters, highlight important topics, and create election narratives.

3.5.4 Partisanship and Media Bias

- News reporting and interpretation may be influenced by the political prejudice shown by media outlets. A partisan public might result from partisan media's presentation of facts in a manner that supports certain political philosophies. This prejudice may influence the representation and comprehension of various political points of view.

- When bias affects media coverage, certain news or viewpoints may be given more attention than others, while others may be minimized or completely disregarded. This biased reporting has the potential to spread false information and distort public opinion.

3.5.5   Social Media's Ascent

- Real-time updates on political events and the quick distribution of information are made possible by social media platforms. While this immediacy might increase public involvement and engagement, it can also aid in the dissemination of false information and unsubstantiated claims.
- Social media may produce echo chambers, where users are mostly exposed to content that confirms their own opinions. This may deepen political division and lessen the range of opinions that people come across.

3.5.6   Control and Censorship

- Traditional and social media platforms may suppress specific material or points of view as part of their content moderation practices. This presents issues with free speech and the repression of opposing viewpoints, even while it may be used to stop offensive or misleading information.
- There are claims that political or governmental figures may use coercion, laws, or overt action to try to shape media narratives. This may have an impact on media outlets' independence and objectivity in reporting.

3.5.7   The Media's Contribution to Political Movements

- Raising public support for political movements or causes may be greatly aided by the media. The media may encourage collective action and elevate voices by providing coverage, analysis, and advocacy.

- Questioning Government Actions and Political power: Media outlets often operate as forums for raising issues with government policies and political power. Ensuring that authority is held responsible and promoting democratic debate are critical functions of this job.

The media has a wide-ranging and significant impact on politics. It includes influencing elections, disseminating information, forming public opinion, and participating in political debate. Although the media may improve democratic accountability and involvement, worries about polarization, prejudice, and censorship draw attention to the difficulties and complexity of the media's position in modern politics. Comprehending these dynamics is crucial in order to effectively navigate the media-politics interface and guarantee the transparency and equity of democratic processes.

3.6   Media bias and misinformation

The integrity of information and public confidence in media institutions are significantly impacted by media bias and disinformation. There are important ramifications for democracy, public opinion, and political processes from both phenomena. This is an analysis of the workings of media bias and disinformation, as well as the effects they have on society:

3.6.1 Recognising Media Bias

The propensity of news organisations to present information in a way that reflects a specific perspective or ideological viewpoint is known as media bias. Political bias, which favors a particular political party or ideology, economic bias, which is motivated by financial interests, and cultural bias, which shapes narratives based on social or cultural values, are examples of different types of bias. Selected reporting, framing, language selections, and editorial choices are some ways that media bias can be shown. For instance, a news organisation may highlight some parts of a story while downplaying others, which could affect how the public views the problem. The public's perception of information is influenced by bias. Political polarization can occur when media outlets continuously present news through a partisan lens, reinforcing preexisting opinions. This selective exposure may create echo chambers where only similar thoughts are heard and hinder people's comprehension of other points of view.

3.6.2 False information

Misinformation includes the spread of erroneous or misleading information without intent to deceive. This might contain faulty data, deceptive figures, or fraudulent assertions. Disinformation, a similar term, is the purposeful fabrication and spread of incorrect information to deceive and manipulate. Misinformation may arise from several sources, including social media, biased news outlets, and people with vested interests. It may spread swiftly via viral material, memes, and unconfirmed claims, especially on sites with inadequate content management. Misinformation may have significant effects, including the loss of faith in media and institutions, the propagation of incorrect views, and the weakening of democratic processes. It may impact public opinion, change voting behavior, and contribute to social instability by fostering confusion and conflict.

3.6.3   The Role of Social Media

Social media platforms facilitate the quick transmission of information, both true and false. The viral nature of social media may perpetuate disinformation, making it hard for consumers to discriminate between credible and dubious sources. Social media algorithms typically emphasise material that fits with users' past interactions, generating echo chambers where people are exposed mostly to information that confirms their current opinions. This may heighten media bias and restrict exposure to alternative opinions.

3.6.4   Addressing Media Bias and Misinformation

Developing critical media literacy skills is vital for navigating biased and misleading information. This requires analysing sources, cross-checking data, and comprehending the possible biases of media outlets. Promoting media literacy education can enable people to choose the information they consume with knowledge. These groups are essential for confirming information and disproving untrue statements. These groups offer useful tools for evaluating the veracity of news and social media content. Media bias can be lessened by promoting ethical journalism practices, such as accountability, fairness, and transparency. To preserve credibility and trust, media outlets should make an effort to present fair reporting and declare any potential conflicts of interest.

3.6.5   The Function of Technology

Search engine and social media algorithms have the power to affect how visible content is. These algorithms frequently give engagement top priority, which occasionally encourages the spread of false or sensationalized information. Fighting for transparency and having an understanding of how these algorithms operate can help stop the spread of false information. New obstacles to recognising and countering misinformation are presented by advances in artificial intelligence, such as deep fake technology. It is vital to develop sophisticated tools for identifying and dealing with digital deception because these technologies have the ability to produce extremely convincing but false content.

In today's information age, media bias and disinformation pose serious problems. Misinformation can erode trust and propagate falsehoods, while media bias can polarize the public and shape public perception. A multifaceted strategy is needed to address these problems, one that includes advancing media literacy, encouraging ethical journalism, and using technology to identify and dispel misleading information. The public can become more informed and involved if society recognises and confronts media bias and disinformation.

3.7   Impact on Public Trust

The interplay between media bias and misinformation has profound effects on public trust in media and institutions. The erosion of trust impacts various aspects of society, including democratic processes, social cohesion, and individual decision-making. Here's an exploration of how media bias and misinformation influence public trust and the broader implications:

3.7.1   Erosion of Trust in Media

When media outlets exhibit bias, whether political, economic, or cultural, it can undermine their perceived credibility. Audiences may begin to question the accuracy and fairness of the information presented, leading to skepticism about the media's reliability. Media bias often reinforces confirmation bias, where individuals seek out information that aligns with their pre-existing beliefs. This can create a cycle where trust is placed in sources that confirm one's views while disregarding those that offer differing perspectives, further polarizing public opinion. The spread of misinformation can exacerbate distrust. As false or misleading information circulates, it undermines confidence in not only the sources of misinformation but also in the media ecosystem as a whole. When individuals are exposed to conflicting reports and unverifiable claims, it becomes challenging to discern what is true, fostering a general sense of distrust.

3.7.2   Impact on Democratic Processes

Trust in media is vital for informed decision-making in democratic society. When media sources are prejudiced or distribute disinformation, it impairs the public's capacity to make well-informed judgements on crucial subjects, including elections and policy affairs. Misinformation campaigns and media bias can influence electoral outcomes by shaping public perceptions of candidates and issues. Election legitimacy can be impacted and democratic processes distorted when voters are tricked or controlled by biased reporting. Political polarization and societal fragmentation are exacerbated by media bias and disinformation. When people are primarily exposed to information that supports their opinions, ideological divisions widen and the possibility of fruitful discussion and consensus-building is diminished.

3.7.3   Public Conversation and Social Cohesion

False information and biased reporting frequently foster divisive narratives that heighten social unrest. Media outlets that highlight divisive or sensational topics have the power to fuel internal conflicts and undermine social cohesiveness. The decline in trust in media can extend to other institutions, including government, academia, and the judiciary. When media sources fail to provide accurate and unbiased information, it can lead to broader skepticism and distrust in societal institutions and their ability to function effectively. Trust in media is integral to active civil engagement. People may become disinterested in politics and less likely to take part in democratic activities like voting and civic engagement when they lose faith in the media's ability to present accurate and fair information.

3.7.4   Individual Decision-Making and Welfare

Misinformation about health and safety issues, such as vaccines or medical treatments, can have direct consequences for public well-being. When individuals are exposed to false information, they may make decisions that jeopardize their health or that of others. Misinformation can also affect financial decisions, including investments and consumer behavior. When media sources present biased or misleading information about economic trends or financial products, it can lead to poor decision-making and financial losses.

3.7.5   Addressing the Impact

Enhancing media literacy skills among the public can help individuals critically evaluate sources, recognize bias, and discern accurate information from misinformation. Education initiatives can empower individuals to make informed judgments about the information they encounter.   Holding media organizations accountable for their reporting practices is essential for restoring public trust. This includes promoting transparency, ethical journalism, and adherence to standards that ensure accuracy and fairness. Collaborative efforts between media organizations, fact-checkers, and technology platforms can help combat misinformation and improve public trust. By correcting disinformation and delivering trustworthy information, these groups may contribute to re-establish faith in the media and associated institutions.

The influence of media bias and disinformation on public trust is extensive and diverse. Eroded confidence undermines democratic processes, societal cohesiveness, and individual decision-making. Addressing these difficulties needs a coordinated effort to educate media literacy, enforce accountability, and develop openness in media operations. By recognising and reducing the consequences of media bias and disinformation, society may strive towards restoring confidence and strengthening the integrity of public debate.

3.8   Rise of alternative media sources

The emergence of alternative media sources marks a substantial change in the media landscape, driven by technology improvements, shifting consumer tastes, and a rising scepticism of established media institutions. This phenomena has revolutionised how information is created, disseminated, and consumed, leading to both possibilities and difficulties for public debate and democracy. Here's an outline of this trend and its implications:

3.8.1 Emergence and Growth of Alternative Media

The emergence of the internet, social media platforms, and mobile technologies has permitted a profusion of alternative media sources. Bloggers, independent journalists, and content producers may now reach global audiences without the need for established media infrastructure.

Platforms such as YouTube, podcasts, social media networks (e.g., Twitter, Facebook, Instagram), and independent news websites have become prominent venues for alternative media. These channels provide a diversity of opinions and coverage on problems that may be underrepresented or misrepresented in mainstream media. The emergence of user-generated material enables people to offer their perspectives, experiences, and research, adding to the variety of accessible knowledge. This democratization of content creation has led to a broader spectrum of voices in the media landscape.

3.8.2 Motivations for Seeking Alternative Media

Growing skepticism towards traditional media outlets, often due to perceived bias, misinformation, or sensationalism, has driven individuals to seek alternative sources for more balanced or different viewpoints. Many consumers turn to alternative media to access unfiltered or uncensored information that they feel is not adequately covered by mainstream outlets. This includes niche topics, investigative journalism, or perspectives that challenge prevailing narratives. Alternative media often fosters a sense of community among its audience, aligning with specific ideologies, interests, or cultural identities. This can create strong bonds between content creators and their audiences, reinforcing engagement and loyalty.

3.8.3 Characteristics of Alternative Media

Alternative media offers a variety of perspectives that conventional media might not always present. Politically conservative or liberal, unusual, or fringe viewpoints can all be a part of this diversity. Rather than relying on traditional advertising revenue, a lot of alternative media sources rely on donations, crowdsourcing, or subscriptions. More editorial freedom may result from this, but it also creates financial dependencies that could affect the content. Long-form articles, interactive content, live streams, and video documentaries are examples of non-traditional content formats in alternative media. The format's adaptability enables a variety of imaginative and inventive approaches to information sharing and storytelling.

3.8.4 Effect on Conversation in Public

The rise of alternative media has broadened access to diverse viewpoints and information, allowing individuals to explore perspectives that may be overlooked by mainstream media.

While alternative media provides diverse viewpoints, it can also contribute to polarization. Audiences may gravitate towards sources that reinforce their existing beliefs, creating echo chambers that exacerbate ideological divides.

3.8.5 Navigating the Alternative Media Landscape

Consumers should critically evaluate alternative media sources, considering factors such as source credibility, evidence-based reporting, and potential biases. Media literacy skills are crucial for discerning reliable information from misinformation. Gaining knowledge from a variety of media sources, including both mainstream and alternative ones, can help you grasp topics more thoroughly. Having a balanced viewpoint makes the public more informed and helps to lessen the impact of echo chambers. Supporting reputable alternative media that adheres to high journalistic standards can help ensure the availability of reliable and diverse information. Encouraging transparency and accountability within alternative media can contribute to maintaining quality and trustworthiness.

3.8.6 Upcoming Patterns

As traditional media outlets adjust to shifting consumer preferences and technological advancements, there's a chance that the increasing influence of alternative media will result in more integration with mainstream media practices. New approaches to information production, distribution, and verification, such as blockchain and artificial intelligence, could influence the direction of alternative media in the future. The emergence of alternative media may bring up issues with ethics, regulations, and the function of platforms in content moderation. Free speech must be balanced with the need to disseminate accurate information.

The emergence of alternative media outlets signifies a noteworthy shift in the media environment, propelled by innovations in technology and evolving consumer inclinations. Alternative media presents issues with polarization, disinformation, and credibility even as it provides chances for a variety of unfiltered and diverse information. Navigating this evolving landscape requires critical evaluation, balanced consumption, and support for quality journalism to ensure a well-informed and engaged public.

CHAPTER NO. 04
THE COVID-19 PANDEMIC

"As John Stuart Mill remarked, 'He who knows only his own side of the case knows little of that.' The COVID-19 pandemic exposed the limitations of our understanding, forcing us to confront the interconnectedness and fragility of our global society."

The SARS-CoV-2 virus, which gave rise to COVID-19, was a worldwide epidemic that had a significant effect on economies, society, and public health. Knowing its beginnings and how it spread will help us better understand how pandemics develop and impact the globe. Origin

In December 2019, Wuhan, in the Chinese province of Hubei, reported the discovery of the new coronavirus. Though some early cases had no direct connection to the market, early instances were associated with a seafood market, which was considered to be a possible source of the virus. SARS-CoV-2 is a member of the coronavirus family, which also contains viruses that cause more serious infections like MERS and SARS as well as ordinary colds. The virus is known for its rapid spread and capacity to infect a variety of people, including carriers who show no symptoms.

Spread

From Wuhan, the virus quickly spread to other parts of China and beyond international boundaries. The World Health Organisation (WHO) declared a public health emergency of international concern on January 30, 2020, and a worldwide pandemic on March 11, 2020, after COVID-19 cases were detected in many countries by January 2020. When an infected individual coughs, sneezes, or speaks, respiratory droplets are the main way that Covid-19 spreads. It is also possible for it to spread by contact with infected surfaces, however this is thought to be a less frequent way. The virus spread quickly because asymptomatic people may pass it to others.

Effect

The symptoms of COVID-19 ranged widely, from minor respiratory problems to severe pneumonia and multiple organ failure. Worldwide healthcare systems were severely strained by the epidemic, which resulted in a scarcity of medical supplies, overcrowded hospitals, and a high death toll. The pandemic caused a great deal of economic upheaval, which included changes in work patterns, job losses, and company closures. To stop the virus's spread, which also impacted everyday life and social connections, governments used a variety of measures, including lockdowns, travel restrictions, and social distance.

Reaction and Modifications

Various tactics were used by nations to contain the virus, including as mass testing, contact tracking, quarantine restrictions, and the creation and dispersal of vaccinations. To prevent transmission, public health initiatives encouraged mask use, good cleanliness, and physical separation. The COVID-19 vaccine was developed at a pace and scale never seen before. A number of vaccines were approved for use in emergency situations or were given complete approval, which prompted vaccination drives throughout the world to manage the epidemic and create herd immunity.

Ongoing Difficulties

The virus's introduction of new strains, such the Delta and Omicron strains, presented new difficulties. Variants have an impact on vaccination effectiveness, public health initiatives, and rates of transmission; as a result, response measures needed to be continuously monitored and adjusted. The pandemic made clear how important it is for nations to work together to manage health emergencies. Controlling the pandemic will still need measures to guarantee fair vaccination distribution and assistance for healthcare systems in low-resource environments.

To sum up, the genesis and dissemination of COVID-19 highlight the intricate dynamics of worldwide pandemics. The rapid spread, major health effects, and wide-ranging social and economic ramifications highlight the difficulties countries have in reacting to a global health emergency.

4.1   Theories and controversies about the origins

4.1.1   Origin of Natural Zoonotic

The most well recognized idea states that COVID-19 started in animals—more especially, bats—and then spread to people.

According to the zoonotic spillover scenario, humans may have acquired the virus from animals via an intermediary host such as pangolins. The similarities of SARS-CoV-2 to other coronaviruses discovered in bats and the known history of zoonotic illnesses lend credence to this notion.

- Coronaviruses discovered in bats and SARS-CoV-2 have a lot in common, according to genetic research. The finding of similar viruses in pangolins supports the intermediate host hypothesis.
- This view is backed by reputable scientific organisations, such as the World Health Organisation (WHO), which points to previous instances of zoonotic transmission in illnesses like SARS and MERS.

4.1.2   The Theory of Laboratory Leaks

According to this scenario, COVID-19 may have unintentionally spilt from a lab where gain-of-function research was done, such the Wuhan Institute of Virology (WIV). Supporters believe that before unintentionally escaping, the virus may have been altered or investigated in a laboratory setting.

- Coronaviruses and the WIV's close proximity to the outbreak's epicenter are two supporting arguments made by some of the advocates. Concerns exist over lab safety procedures as well.
- Although some of the early hypotheses were disproved, fresh research and discussions have maintained this hypothesis at the forefront. Nevertheless, this notion is still being researched since there is currently no concrete evidence to support it.

4.1.3   Theory of Bioweapons

According to this idea, SARS-CoV-2 was purposefully created and disseminated as a bioweapon. This theory's proponents contend that the virus's unique properties imply it may have been created with biological warfare in mind.

- Experts have mostly discounted the hypothesis since there is insufficient evidence to prove intentional manufacture or release. There are no indications of intentional modification in the virus's genetic composition.

- According to the majority of scientists, SARS-CoV-2 does not exhibit any characteristics that would suggest it is a bioweapon, so they reject this notion. For the most part, the hypothesis is dismissed as a hoax without solid proof.

4.1.4   The Wet Market's Function

Early cases were connected to Wuhan's Huainan Seafood Wholesale Market, which was first suggested as a potential epidemic site. According to this argument, tainted animals sold at the market may have carried the virus, which might then have spread to people.

- Several of the first COVID-19 cases were connected to the market, according to early reports, which sparked conjecture regarding the market's involvement in the epidemic.

- Investigations further revealed that while the market could have served as an amplification location, it might not have been the source. The market may not have been the original source of the virus, but rather a place where it propagated, according to early instances connected to it.

4.1.5   Alternative Hypotheses and Conjectures

Other ideas have surfaced, speculating that the virus may have come from other parts of the world or involved different animal hosts.

- These hypotheses often lack strong scientific support and are based on little or conjectural evidence.
- Other ideas are usually regarded as speculative or lacking significant evidence, whereas the majority of scientists and researchers endorse the zoonotic origin explanation.

4.1.6   Exams and Present Situation

- The WHO looked into the origins of the virus, working in conjunction with Chinese experts on one research. Although a zoonotic origin was determined to be more probable, the lab-leak scenario was not completely discounted.
- In order to get a deeper understanding of the origins of SARS-CoV-2, further study is being conducted on animal reservoirs, the significance of certain wildlife species, and laboratory safety procedures.

The discussion around the origins of COVID-19 is part of a larger attempt to understand the emergence of pandemics and avoid them in the future. Even though the zoonotic hypothesis is still the most widely accepted, further studies and research are necessary to ensure clarity and worldwide readiness.

4.2   Government and Media Response

4.2.1   Government Response to COVID-19

Initial Reactions

China: At first, the Chinese authorities played down how serious the epidemic was. Wuhan was the source of the first reports of the virus, but local officials delayed disclosing the true scope of the danger. The epidemic was reported to the World Health Organisation (WHO) by Chinese authorities in December 2019, but it took several weeks for the situation to be declared a worldwide emergency.

Global Reaction: As the virus spread, nations all over the globe started taking different actions. On January 30, 2020, the WHO classified COVID-19 as a Public Health Emergency of International Concern (PHEIC), and on March 11, 2020, it was classified as a pandemic.

National Reactions

United States: The government of the United States was first criticized for its tardiness in responding. The Trump administration ordered lockdowns and social distancing measures, imposed visa restrictions from China, and proclaimed a national emergency. As part of Operation Warp Speed, the U.S. federal government distributed personal protective equipment (PPE), implemented stimulus packages, and developed and distributed vaccinations quickly.

Europe: Different reactions were seen in different European nations. Early on, countries like Italy and Spain were severely affected, which resulted in strict lockdowns and stress on the healthcare system. The

European Union supported its member states financially and coordinated efforts to obtain and distribute vaccinations.

Other Countries: Governments throughout the world used a variety of tactics, ranging from forceful lockdowns and testing to focused limitations and public health initiatives. Nations that effectively managed the problem via stringent border restrictions and early interventions were New Zealand and Taiwan.

Public Health Measures:

Lockdowns and Quarantines: Lockdowns were imposed in several nations to restrict travel and lessen the spread of disease. Depending on the level of healthcare availability and local infection rates, these measures varied in length and intensity.

Testing and Contact Tracing: These two essential strategies for controlling epidemics were widely used. Governments spent money testing technologies and infrastructure to monitor and stop the virus's spread.

Vaccination Campaigns: A major emphasis of government efforts shifted to the development and distribution of vaccinations. Globally, mass immunization efforts were implemented with differing degrees of success and difficulties.

4.2.2   Media Response to COVID

Timely Reporting:

Early attention: The Wuhan epidemic and its potential worldwide expansion were the main topics of early media attention. The seriousness of the illness and the reactions of the medical community and governments were emphasised in reports.

Misinformation: Early on, rumors and false information circulated alongside factual news, which added to the public's anxiety and bewilderment. False information on the virus's causes, cures, and preventative measures were among them.

Changing Narratives

Emphasis on Health Effects: As the pandemic spread, media attention was progressively more focused on COVID-19's health effects, including case counts, hospitalization rates, and mortality rates. Accounts of the experiences of healthcare professionals and patient outcomes gained popularity.

Political and Economic Aspects: Media sources started examining the pandemic's political and economic aspects, including the effects on different sectors, government reactions, and the aftermath on the economy. Debates over stimulus packages, lockdowns, and the efficacy of pandemic control techniques were covered.

Rebukes and Difficulties:

Media Bias: The media has often come under fire for its alleged bias, with certain publications being charged with sensationalizing the epidemic or endorsing specific political positions. Depending on the viewpoint of the publication, different government actions and health initiatives were portrayed in very different ways.

Censorship and disinformation: Social media companies came under fire for their attempts to filter false claims and for their part in the dissemination of disinformation. It became controversial to strike a balance between policing content and guaranteeing free expression.

Effect on Public Opinion:

Institutional Trust: Public perceptions of health institutions and government actions were impacted by media coverage. Confusion and mistrust were exacerbated by contradictory information and inconsistent communications.

Awareness and Engagement: The media was essential in spreading public health initiatives and increasing awareness about COVID-19. Public education campaigns and information-sharing initiatives were designed to teach people about vaccinations, safety precautions, and the value of following health recommendations.

The way the people saw and dealt with the COVID-19 epidemic was influenced by the way the government and media handled the situation. Lockdowns, vaccination campaigns, and public health initiatives were among the government's key initiatives in halting the virus's spread. Even though media coverage is essential for spreading information, prejudice, false information, and public trust were issues that it had to deal with. The dynamic between official reactions and media representations brought to light the difficulties in overseeing a worldwide health emergency and the need of precise and unambiguous communication during emergencies.

4.3   Media coverage and public reaction

4.3.1   Media Coverage

Intensity and Focus:

- 24/7 News Cycle: News coverage globally was dominated by the COVID-19 epidemic. Public health standards, government actions, and infection rates were constantly updated by media sources. The public was kept interested and informed by the constant news cycle that resulted from the increased attention on the outbreak.

- Traditional news networks, digital media, and social media were among the outlets from which coverage differed. Every platform had a different tack when it came to covering the epidemic, which affected how the public saw and comprehended it.

Stressing Conflict and Crisis:

- By emphasizing growing case counts, overburdened healthcare systems, and heartbreaking human accounts, media coverage often emphasised the pandemic's severity. The goal of emphasizing crisis reporting was to draw attention to how severe the situation was and to encourage people to follow health recommendations.

- The media also discussed and debated the merits of lockdowns, mask laws, and vaccination campaigns, among other pandemic preparedness measures. These discussions often polarized public opinion and stoked controversy fuelled by the media.

Government and Expert Reporting:

- To inform the public about pandemic developments, governments and health organisations regularly hosted press conferences and briefings. The dissemination of official information and directives was greatly aided by the media's coverage of these briefings.

- In media coverage, scientists, epidemiologists, and health professionals regularly offered their opinions on the behaviour of the virus, available treatments, and the creation of vaccines. Adherence to health measures required public confidence in these experts.

Criticism and Scrutiny

- Media outlets closely examined the government's reactions to the pandemic, focusing on the timeliness of vaccine deployment, the efficacy of lockdown measures, and the suitability of testing. In media coverage, criticism of government management was a recurring subject.
- One major problem with the epidemic was the dissemination of false information and conspiracy theories. Media organisations struggled to provide accurate and trustworthy news while battling misinformation.

4.3.2   Public Response:

Adherence and Compliance:

- The public's response to media coverage varied, but many people complied with the stated health limitations and recommendations. The media's depiction of the pandemic's severity and the significance of lockdowns, social distance, and mask-wearing impacted compliance with these measures.
- Some people and organisations disapproved of health recommendations and lockdown procedures, sometimes as a result of mistrust of government activities or media coverage. Sometimes contradicting facts and apparent flaws in media coverage fuelled public resentment.

Fear and Anxiety:

- The pandemic's media coverage added to the general worry and anxiety. Concern for the personal and family health of the public increased due to ongoing reporting on the growing number of cases, hospitalizations, and deaths.

- Stress, sadness, and anxiety were among the major effects on mental health that the epidemic and its media coverage had. The way the epidemic was portrayed as a worldwide emergency made people feel more scared and apprehensive.

Polarization and Debate

- The epidemic was often covered by polarized media, which reflected and widened already-existing political divisions. Political circumstances were often used to frame discussions about pandemic measures, such mask requirements and lockdowns, which influenced public perceptions and responses.

- The public's response to the epidemic was greatly influenced by social media platforms. Conspiracy theories, false information, and the quick dissemination of knowledge all influenced the public's reactions and polarized opinions.

- The public's demand for transparency and accountability increased as a result of the media's emphasis on government responses and expert opinions. People demanded clear, consistent information and held authorities responsible for how they handled the pandemic.

- Public confidence in government agencies and the media was impacted by media coverage. While some people believed what the government said, others questioned the veracity and motivations of news reports and official actions.

Public opinion and response to the COVID-19 pandemic were significantly influenced by media coverage of the outbreak. Public perception and adherence to health measures were affected by the increased attention on crisis reporting, contentious problems, and government response. Even while the media tried to enlighten and educate the public, it also increased tension, division, and scrutiny. The intricate interactions between public opinion and media coverage underscore the difficulties in disseminating knowledge and maintaining confidence in the face of a worldwide health emergency.

4.4   Impact on the 2020 Election

The 2020 U.S. presidential election was significantly impacted by the COVID-19 epidemic, which also changed voter behaviour and public opinion. This is a thorough summary of its effects:

4.4.1   Election Procedure and Arrangements:

Mail-In Voting:

- Voters opted to forego in-person polling places during the epidemic, which resulted in a notable rise in mail-in and absentee ballots. Concerns concerning COVID-19 transmission and safety were the main drivers of this spike.
- A number of states have enacted differing mail-in voting procedures, such as extending deadlines and broadening eligibility. As a result, the nation's electoral environment became complicated and unequal.

Changes to the Polling Location:

- In response to the pandemic, a number of polling locations instituted social distance, mask requirements, and sanitization procedures as health and safety precautions. This created logistical difficulties while simultaneously trying to safeguard poll workers and voters.
- Due to personnel shortages and health issues, several polling stations were closed or combined, which may have affected voter access and turnout.

4.4.2   Campaign Strategies and Messaging:

- Transition to Online Platforms: Due to social distance, politicians were forced to use virtual campaigning in place of conventional campaign rallies and events. To engage voters, this includes holding virtual town halls, holding rallies virtually, and interacting on social media.
- Both campaigns stepped up their attempts to reach voters online, including email campaigns, social media platforms, and online advertisements.

Health and Economic message:

The pandemic had an impact on the candidates' campaign message, as they emphasised how they would handle COVID-19 and deal with its financial consequences. While the Biden campaign chastised Trump for his handling of the epidemic and pledged a better coordinated response, the Trump team emphasised its efforts to reopen the economy and deliver vaccinations. The pandemic's effects on the economy made it a major campaign topic. Economic recovery plans, company closures, and unemployment rates were hot subjects of conversation.

4.4.3 Voter Perception and Behaviour:

A key topic in the election was President Trump's management of the epidemic. His administration's reaction, which was closely examined and turned into a target for opponents, including the early downplaying of the virus, shortages of testing, and conflicting messages.

Biden's Criticism:

Joe Biden expressed his disapproval of Trump's handling and inadequacy of the pandemic response. Managing COVID-19 requires a more comprehensive and scientific strategy, as shown by Biden's campaign.

Priorities of Voters:

As a result of the epidemic, a lot of voters now prioritise health care and pandemic management while casting their ballots. Voters' worries were impacted by the pandemic's effects on the economy, and many of them looked for a candidate who could handle the financial difficulties brought on by COVID-19.

4.4.4 Media Coverage and Public Discourse

Media Focus:

The news cycle before the election was dominated by media coverage of the pandemic. Voters' perceptions of the candidates' answers to the crisis were impacted by this wide coverage, which also altered public conversation. With contrasting accounts of the virus's severity and the efficacy of the response, the media's depiction of the pandemic and its effects on the election led to political polarization.

False and Misleading Information

The public's impression of COVID-19 was damaged by the dissemination of false information and disinformation, including conspiracy theories and unsubstantiated allegations, which further polarized and confused the election. Following the election, allegations of fraud and false information about mail-in votes raised serious concerns around election integrity.

4.4.5 Election Outcomes and Repercussions

High Turnout: A record number of people cast ballots in the 2020 election, in part due to a surge in early and mail-in voting. The epidemic made voting even more crucial and encouraged a large turnout of voters to cast ballots. After the election, there were legal challenges, claims of voter fraud, and disagreements about how mail-in votes were handled. These debates were exacerbated by the voting process's modifications brought forth by the epidemic.

The 2020 U.S. presidential election was significantly impacted by the COVID-19 epidemic, which also had an influence on voter behaviour, campaign tactics, media coverage, and the electoral process. The epidemic changed voter priorities, impacted how the public saw the candidates, and created new difficulties for the political process. As a consequence, the election captured the extraordinary difficulties of a worldwide health crisis in addition to the political environment.

4.5   Modifications to the voting process

Significant modifications to voting processes for the 2020 U.S. presidential election were brought about by the COVID-19 epidemic. These changes attempted to meet the particular difficulties brought up by the epidemic while guaranteeing voter safety and accessibility. Here is a thorough analysis of the main adjustments:

4.5.1   Expansion of Mail-In and Absentee Voting

A number of states extended mail-in and absentee voting options to voters unable or unable to cast ballots in person because of health issues. This included adjustments to the criteria for eligibility and the application procedure. This option, which allows voters to request a mail-in ballot without giving a particular reason for missing in person voting, was introduced or expanded in several states. Ballot Request and Delivery: Election officials in each locality might accept requests for mail-in ballots, which would then be delivered to the voters. Many states changed their deadlines for seeking and returning votes to account for the increased demand.

Voters may trace the progress of their mail-in votes thanks to ballot tracking systems that have been developed in numerous states in response to concerns about ballot security and delivery.

4.5.2   Modifications to In-Person Polling

To lower the danger of Covid-19 transmission, polling venues employed social distancing measures. This included setting up polling places such that there would be enough space between voters. Personal Protective Equipment (PPE), Masks and hand sanitizers were either mandated or recommended for poll workers and voters.

Additionally, polling places were regularly cleaned and disinfected to maintain hygiene. Modifications to Polling Locations, Owing to logistical issues, personnel shortages, or health concerns, certain polling stations were closed or combined. Voters sometimes have to go further or wait longer as a consequence of this. To meet growing demand and relieve congestion at polling places, some jurisdictions have extended voting hours.

4.5.3   Drop boxes and early voting

To decrease the number of voters who must cast ballots on Election Day, some states expanded their early voting sessions. Voters now have more time and flexibility to cast their votes as a result. Secure Drop Boxes: Many jurisdictions constructed secure drop boxes where voters may turn in their completed mail-in ballots in order to ease mail-in voting and assure secure ballot submission. This reduced the possibility of vote manipulation and postal delays.

4.5.4   Registration and Validation of Voters

To make it simpler for voters to register or update their registration information without needing to physically visit a registration office, a number of states have increased or encouraged online voter registration. In an effort to accommodate last-minute modifications and guarantee that more voters could participate, some jurisdictions extended their deadlines for voter registration or permitted same-day registration in reaction to the epidemic. Strict protocols for confirming signatures on mail-in ballots were put in place by states that adopted mail-in voting in order to guard against fraud and guarantee the fairness of the electoral process. Voters often have the chance to fix any problems with their ballots.

4.5.5 Modifications to Law and Policy

A number of legal issues arose in response to the voting method modifications, including disagreements on the validity and execution of expanding mail-in voting and making modifications to in-person voting procedures. Courts rendered decisions that influenced the scope and character of the modifications, resulting in different state-by-state protocols and sometimes creating misunderstandings among voters and election officials. Guidelines and suggestions for handling the election in the midst of the epidemic were given by federal and state authorities. The Centers for Disease Control and Prevention (CDC) provided advice on safe voting procedures and public health initiatives in this.

Significant modifications to voting processes were required for the 2020 election due to the COVID-19 outbreak in order to ensure accessibility and safeguard voter health. The extension of mail-in and absentee voting, alterations to in-person voting protocols, and tweaks to early voting and voter registration procedures were some of these improvements. Although these modifications were made to meet the needs of the epidemic, they also brought additional procedural and legal difficulties to the election process.

4.6 Allegations of manipulation and fraud

Many claims of fraud and electoral tampering surrounded the 2020 U.S. presidential election. There has been a great deal of discussion and investigation around these claims, which has heightened tensions in the political environment. Below is a detailed synopsis of the main accusations:

4.6.1   Election Fraud Allegations

According to some detractors, the rise in mail-in voting has made voter fraud more likely. There were accusations of votes being tampered with or changed, ballots being delivered to the wrong addresses, and the same individual casting several ballots. Several audits and investigations were carried out to substantiate these assertions. No proof of massive voting fraud was discovered in the majority of these investigations. For example, according to a thorough analysis conducted by the Cybersecurity and Infrastructure Security Agency (CISA), the 2020 election was among the safest in American history.

It was alleged that votes were cast on behalf of persons who had passed away or who were not allowed to vote, such as foreign nationals. Voter rolls were allegedly inaccurately maintained, according to some. Several state and municipal election authorities' reports revealed that there was insufficient proof to back up these assertions. Reviewing voter registers and confirming eligibility did not turn up any notable cases of fraud.

4.6.2   Hacking of Voting Machines

It was alleged that voting machines were tampered with in order to change the vote totals. Software bugs, hacking, and deliberate manipulation by foreign or local players were among the theories put forward. There was no proof of any tampering or manipulation discovered during independent audits and technical assessments of voting devices. The integrity of the electoral infrastructure was validated by the U.S. Department of Homeland Security and other authorities. Particularly, Dominion Voting Systems, a provider of election equipment, came under fire but refuted the accusations with documentation and legal action.

It was alleged that some voting machine software, including Dominion and Smartmatic, had flaws that might be used to rig elections. Experts and authorities disputed these allegations, asserting that no weaknesses or indications of manipulation existed. A dearth of evidence led to the dismissal of many court proceedings pertaining to these charges.

4.6.3 Irregularities and problems with procedure

According to some observers, poll watchers were not allowed to see the votes being counted, raising questions over the validity and transparency of the vote count. Although there were a few isolated cases of procedural problems, reviews and audits carried out in different states found that they had no effect on the election's general integrity. Legal actions and remedial actions addressed a number of issues. There have been allegations of mismatched signatures, improper handling of ballots, and delays in the reporting of results. After examining these allegations, election authorities and impartial observers found no proof of systemic fraud. Recounts and audits were used to remedy any procedural mistakes found.

4.6.4 Legal Disputes and Court Decisions

Several lawsuits claiming fraud and contesting the election's results were filed after it. These lawsuits, which were brought in a number of states, aimed to annul or contest the election's outcome. Due to insufficient evidence or procedural problems, the courts rejected the great majority of these claims. The Supreme Court and other national courts were unable to uncover enough evidence to reverse the election results. To confirm the correctness of the vote totals, recounts were carried out in significant swing states. These recollections supported the first findings and turned up no proof of fraud. After conducting post-election audits, some states discovered no anomalies that may have an impact on the results. The correctness and integrity of the election results were confirmed by audits.

4.6.5   Effect and Public Opinion

The claims of fraud and manipulation exacerbated division and misplaced confidence in the election system. The public's trust in democratic institutions and elections has been negatively impacted for a long time by this. Public perceptions of voting and election integrity, legislation, and political debate have all been impacted by the 2020 election dispute.

The 2020 U.S. presidential election was the target of several accusations of fraud and manipulation. These charges included accusations of ballot counting problems, voting machine manipulation, abnormalities in the voting process, and voter fraud. Most of these allegations were unsupported by evidence, even after thorough investigations, audits, and court cases. The election results were maintained, and the security and accuracy of the processes were verified. Nonetheless, the public's opinion of and confidence in the election system have been significantly impacted by the dispute.

Chapter No. 05
The 2020 Election – Controversy and Aftermath

"As Friedrich Nietzsche noted, 'In individuals, insanity is rare; but in groups, parties, nations and epochs, it is the rule.' The 2020 election controversy reminded us that mass movements and collective decisions often defy rationality and clear judgment, leading to deep societal divisions."

There was a great deal of controversy and disagreement around the 2020 US presidential election. Allegations of extensive voter fraud, voting machine manipulation, and abnormalities in the procedures sparked significant investigation and legal challenges. Allegations continued despite many investigations and recounts verifying the election's integrity, which exacerbated political division and popular distrust of democratic institutions. Following the event, discussions over election integrity persisted, which had an effect on American political discourse and confidence in voting procedures. One of the distinguishing characteristics of modern American politics is the turmoil surrounding the election.

5.1   The Election Campaign

One of the most divisive and well-publicized presidential campaigns in modern American history was the 2020 one. During the campaign, current President Donald Trump and former Vice President Joe Biden engaged in a fierce rivalry based on their diametrically opposed visions for the nation. This chapter examines the salient features of the campaign, such as the main tactics, critical incidents, and general climate as the two contenders fought for the president.

Principal Techniques and Crucial Times Trump's Political Manoeuvres: Appeals to his core supporters and strengthening his base were key components of President Trump's campaign approach. With a focus on deregulation, robust immigration policies, and economic development, Trump sought to galvanize supporters fed up with the current quo. His strategy comprised:

- Rallies and Media Presence: To energies his supporters, Trump used his charm and in-person interactions with people to host sizable rallies around the nation. Additionally, he continued to be very active in the media, communicating with the people directly via Twitter and other channels rather than through conventional media.

- "Law and Order" Messaging: In reaction to demonstrations and civil upheaval, Trump focused his campaign around questions of law and order. In opposition to what he saw as extreme leftist objectives, he positioned himself as a champion of American ideals and stability.

- Economic Achievements: In order to establish Trump as a prosperous businessman with the ability to boost the economy, the campaign emphasised the pre-pandemic economic growth, low unemployment rates, and tax cuts.

- Joe Biden, the former vice president, used contrast and recuperation as his main campaign themes. Among his tactics were:

- Emphasis on Unity and Decency: In contrast to Trump's divisive comments, Biden centred his campaign on bringing unity and decency back to the presidency. In the midst of escalating political unrest, he presented himself as a uniting force that could unite Americans.

- COVID-19 Reaction: Biden denounced the way the Trump administration was managing the COVID-19 outbreak, contending that a new head of state was required to successfully handle the situation. During his campaign, a thorough strategy for stopping the epidemic and fostering economic recovery was pushed.

- Digital Campaigning and Outreach: In order to reach voters, Biden's campaign depended more and more on digital technologies, virtual events, and targeted advertising as the COVID-19 epidemic restricted in-person activities. To interact with voters, the campaign stressed internet engagement and grassroots mobilization.

5.1.2   Pivotal Moments and Events

Debates and Public Appearances

On September 29, 2020, Trump and Biden participated in their first debate, which was characterised by a number of interruptions and acerbic exchanges. It emphasised how drastically different the platforms and philosophies of the two candidates were, with Trump taking a more assertive stance and Biden trying to maintain composure. On October 7, 2020, Mike Pence and Kamala Harris engaged in a discussion that attracted a lot of interest. Pence was directly questioned by Harris throughout her performance on topics such as racial justice and the epidemic, while Pence defended the administration's record.

Early voting and mail-in ballots saw a notable spike as a result of the epidemic. Both camps modified their approaches in response to the shifting circumstances, with Trump's team voicing doubts about the validity of mail-in ballots and Biden's campaign promoting early voting.

Election Day: The Repercussions Both campaigns had difficulties on Election Day with regard to voter participation and ballot counting. Trump's team contested the results and made accusations of fraud, which heightened tensions and created a tense aftermath after the protracted counting process in crucial battleground states.

The 2020 election campaign was characterised by extreme polarization and enormous stakes. To appeal to their supporters and address the pressing challenges of the day, such as the epidemic and social instability, both candidates used different tactics. The election season profoundly altered the political environment by laying the groundwork for the divisive and combative post-election era.

5.2   The impact of COVID-19 on campaigning

The COVID-19 epidemic had a significant impact on the 2020 election campaign, changing conventional campaign strategies and influencing voter behaviour. Both efforts had to immediately adjust to a rapidly changing environment as the virus spread.

5.2.1   Shift to Digital and Virtual Campaigning

Both campaigns used virtual events and webinars to interact with voters in the wake of social distancing measures and limitations on mass gatherings. Online town halls and campaign rallies gave politicians the opportunity to contact audiences without being physically confined. Specifically, Biden's campaign used Zoom conversations and live streamed events to communicate with supporters and recruit volunteers. The epidemic hastened the use of social media as the main channel for political discourse. Trump and Biden both made more appearances on social media sites including Facebook, Instagram, and Twitter. Digital advertisements, with their focused message designed to allay fears about COVID-19 and advance political narratives, have emerged as an indispensable instrument for reaching voters. Due to the decline of conventional fundraising events, internet fundraising initiatives have become crucial. Both campaigns made use of internet channels to generate money, soliciting donations via email campaigns, social media appeals, and virtual fundraisers.

5.2.2   Changes in Voter Behavior and Campaign Tactics

The epidemic contributed to a notable rise in early and mail-in voting. Many voters choose these options due to worries about polling place safety and in-person voting. In order to encourage early voting and solve anticipated problems with mail-in votes, campaigns had to modify their tactics. While Trump's team expressed doubts about the integrity of mail-in voting, Biden's campaign placed special emphasis on the value of voting early and by mail.

COVID-19 caused the campaign's emphasis to change to public health and safety concerns. In addition to outlining a thorough crisis management strategy, Biden's campaign attacked the Trump administration's handling of the outbreak. The Trump campaign placed a strong emphasis on economic recovery and reopening measures while defending the administration's performance. Regarding their reactions to the epidemic and their strategies for future public health initiatives, both candidates came under intense scrutiny. Strict restrictions were placed on conventional voter outreach techniques including door-to-door canvassing and in-person rallies. Both campaigns adjusted by depending more on text messaging, phone banking, and online canvassing. In order to reach voters and promote engagement, the Biden campaign, in particular, placed a strong emphasis on grassroots digital mobilization.

5.2.3   Public Response and Modifications

Enhanced Online Voter Engagement Online engagement increased as a consequence of the switch to digital campaigning. Social media users grew more engaged, exchanging information, debating campaign topics, and taking part in online events. The public's view and interaction with the candidates were impacted by this surge in internet activity. Additional difficulties were brought about by the use of internet campaigning and mail-in voting. Controversial topics included mail-in ballot delays, allegations of fraud, and internet platform security. Both campaigns overcame these obstacles while addressing issues with voter access and election integrity.

The 2020 election campaign was drastically altered by the COVID-19 epidemic, which led to a move towards digital and virtual means of campaigning and influencing voter behaviour. To varied degrees, both contenders adjusted to the new circumstances. The epidemic brought attention to the significance of adaptability and creativity in political campaigns as well as the influence of outside variables on election procedures.

5.3   Election Night and Results

5.3.1   First Anticipations and Crucial States

There was a great deal of excitement and uncertainty on Election Night 2020 as ballots were being counted all around the nation. There were high hopes for a clear winner going into the event, but as the evening wore on, it became clear how complicated the election results were.

As polls closed around the country, it seemed that President Donald Trump had established an early lead in a number of crucial battleground states, such as Florida, Ohio, and Texas. At first, Trump was favored by these states, which were critical for a winning route, which encouraged his fans.

In contrast, states like Pennsylvania, Michigan, and Wisconsin had a slower pace of mail-in and absentee vote counting. Owing to the pandemic, a significant portion of voters chose to cast mail-in votes, which required more time to complete. As the results started to come in, the situation changed as a consequence of the counting delay.

5.3.2   Developments and Shifts

As the evening wore on, the outcomes started to change. The lead started to close in areas where Trump had an early advantage, including Pennsylvania and Michigan, as more mail-in votes were tabulated. This movement was explained by the fact that a large number of Democrats had shifted to mail-in voting, which progressively tipped the scales in these pivotal states. In crucial battleground states, Vice President Joe Biden saw a late increase in support. His campaign placed a strong emphasis on early and mail-in voting, and as a consequence, these ballots started to have a big influence on the final outcome. In states that were critical to winning the Electoral College, Biden started to close the gap on Trump late into the night and early the next morning.

5.3.3   Media Forecasts and Responses

On Election Night, the public's perspective was greatly influenced by the media's predictions. With the data at hand, networks like CNN and NBC started to project states. At first, forecasts for states like Pennsylvania and Georgia started to move towards Biden, but as more ballots were collected, Trump's position was predicted to be solid. On Election Night, there was a mix of uncertainty and worry among the public. As the results changed, supporters of both candidates felt both optimism and sadness. Real-time reports, accusations, and denials about the integrity and precision of the vote-counting procedure were all over social media.

5.3.4   Important Events and Outcomes

Several states were too close to call as the evening wore on. Particularly, Georgia and Arizona were crucial in deciding how things turned out in the end. As more ballots were tabulated, Biden's campaign gained momentum and Trump's advantage in these states shrank.

When media outlets started predicting Pennsylvania would support Biden, it was the tipping point. This prediction, along with the outcomes from other significant states, confirmed Biden's winning trajectory. Biden was announced as the 2020 presidential winner in the early hours of November 7, 2020.

5.3.4   Aftermath and Immediate Reactions

The Joe Biden campaign released a statement expressing gratitude for the win, highlighting its importance, and urging cooperation. In his victory speech, Biden addressed the profound differences that had marked the race by emphasizing themes of healing and reconciliation.

Despite the results, President Trump and his campaign disputed them, claiming massive voting fraud and anomalies. The Trump team claimed that the election had been rigged and launched many lawsuits as well as requests for recounts in various states. These allegations laid the groundwork for the protracted post-election dispute and ensuing legal disputes.

Election Night 2020 revealed the intricacies of a fiercely fought and first-ever election with abrupt changes and dynamic outcomes. Trump's early advantage and Biden's late comeback highlighted the significance of mail-in votes and the difficulties of an election in a pandemic period. An important turning point was the final projection of Biden as the victor, which sparked continued discussions and legal challenges that affected the weeks that followed.

5.4   Initial results and media coverage

5.4.1   Initial Results

As polls closed nationwide on Election Night, preliminary findings showed that President Donald Trump had performed well in a number of crucial battleground states early on. Early results from states like Florida, Ohio, and Texas looked to favor Trump, which gave his supporters further optimism. Early tallies indicated that Trump was ahead in key states including Pennsylvania, Michigan, Wisconsin, and Georgia, mostly as a result of in-person votes cast on Election Day. Early results seemed to point to a clean win for Trump, but there was still a considerable amount of mail-in and absentee votes that needed to be tallied, which muddied the picture.

5.4.2   Media Coverage

Throughout the evening, the media significantly influenced how the general public saw the situation. Based on early results, early predictions from networks including CNN, Fox News, and NBC represented Trump's strong showing. Because of the media's focus on these first estimates, a narrative emerged that suggested Trump would win important states; this narrative was extensively covered and debated on social media. As the evening wore on, the media's portrayal started to change. Early leads were shifted in emphasis to the changing mail-in and absentee ballot totals. News outlets started to report that most mail-in votes—most of which were submitted by Democrats—were still pending tallying. This change in emphasis brought attention to the increasing ambiguity and shifting dynamics of the race.

The media gave constant updates on how each state's vote tally was progressing. The media focused on the shifting margins as these votes were counted, particularly for states like Pennsylvania, Michigan, and Georgia where vote counting was slowed down by the amount of mail-in ballots. The idea that the race was becoming closer was aided by the media's emphasis on the outcomes of these states.

5.4.3 Key Moments in Media Coverage

Early in the evening, media sources indicated that Trump was ahead in a number of states that are considered battlegrounds. The first stories included headlines and images portraying Trump as having a firm stance. Trump gained momentum as a result of this coverage, which was mirrored in the responses of his followers. As the evening went on and more mail-in votes were tallied, the media's portrayal started to alter to reflect the evolving situation. According to reports, the lead in a number of important states was changing as a result of the vote counting. For example, Biden's numbers started to rise when more mail-in votes were tabulated in Georgia and Pennsylvania, which caused the media to change its emphasis. Early on November 7, 2020, media sources started predicting that Joe Biden would win Pennsylvania and the election as a whole. Based on the latest numbers and the shrinking margins in important states, this forecast was made. The media's prediction was important because it signaled a change in how the election was portrayed.

5.4.4 Reactions from the Public

The public's response to the media coverage was not uniform. While supporters of Biden experienced concern as the counts progressed, supporters of Trump were initially encouraged by the early results and media estimates. There was a mixture of excitement and bewilderment on both sides as the outcomes in crucial states started to change. The proliferation of allegations and denials about the election was greatly aided by social media. Posts on social media sites challenging the validity of the vote-counting procedure increased as a consequence of media coverage of the shifting results. These postings added to the escalating uproar by often including claims of anomalies and voting fraud. Election Night 2020's preliminary results and media coverage paved the way for a shocking and divisive conclusion. Early predictions were for a strong showing for Trump, but as mail-in votes were counted, the storylines changed, and Biden was finally predicted to win. The way the people responded to these events and how the media covered they brought attention to the intricacies and unpredictability's of the election, hinting at the arguments and controversies that would follow.

5.5   Allegations of election fraud

Significant charges of election fraud surfaced after the 2020 presidential election, originating from a number of sources, including former President Donald Trump, his allies, and some conservative media sites. These accusations centred on matters pertaining to the validity of mail-in votes, the integrity of the vote-counting procedure, and other procedural difficulties. Following the election, the dispute around these allegations took center stage and had an impact on both public opinion and legal actions.

5.5.1   Principal Allegations and Claims

The main accusation was that the vote-counting procedure included anomalies. Trump supporters said that there were occasions when monitors were reportedly excluded from seeing the count and that the counting process was opaque in a number of crucial battleground states.

Mail-in ballots were the subject of another significant allegation. There were allegations of fraudulent or multiple voting, that these votes were handled inappropriately, and that some were mailed out or received beyond the dates set by law. Some said that the mail-in voting procedure was susceptible to fraud and that there were anomalies in the signature verification procedure.

It has been alleged that software and voting equipment have been tampered with or malfunctioned, resulting in erroneous vote tallies. There have been allegations that software used to count the ballots was flawed or that certain computers were manipulated to change votes from Trump to Biden. There were additional allegations of voting list inaccuracies, including the accusation that votes were tallied for dead people, non-citizens, or those who had moved out of the jurisdiction.

5.5.2   Legal and Inquiry Reactions

Following the election, a number of lawsuits were launched in many important states by Trump and his associates contesting the results. The purpose of these cases was to remedy alleged fraud and anomalies. But the majority of these legal challenges were rejected by the courts on the grounds of insufficient evidence or improper procedure. A number of states looked into the fraud charges. For instance, states like Georgia and Arizona conducted audits and recounts. These investigations mostly supported the preliminary findings, finding no convincing proof of widespread fraud.

In spite of the accusations, the Department of Justice and the Cybersecurity and Infrastructure Security Agency (CISA), among other federal and state agencies, certified that the election was legitimate and that there was no proof that widespread fraud had affected the results. Officials from the state, representing both the Democratic and Republican parties, confirmed the accuracy of their certifications and vote tallies.

5.5.3   Influence and Public View

The claims of electoral manipulation intensified political division in the US. The allegations stoked widespread mistrust in the voting system by motivating many Trump supporters to believe that the election was rigged. On the other hand, a lot of detractors thought these assertions were baseless and a danger to democratic values. The claims were extensively covered by the media. While mainstream media often concentrated on refuting allegations of fraud and reporting on the absence of supporting data, conservative media sources frequently emphasised and magnified such accusations. Further disarray and uncertainty were exacerbated by this inconsistent media portrayal. In the years that followed the 2020 election, discussions and legislative actions pertaining to voting processes and election security were impacted by the controversy surrounding the election and the accusations of fraud that followed. In reaction to the discussions around election integrity, some states amended their election laws.

The claims of election fraud in the 2020 presidential contest gained significant attention, affecting public confidence in the democratic process and escalating social and political tensions. Although most of the allegations of massive fraud were not supported by investigations or legal challenges, the scandal had a lasting impact on public debate on election integrity and the political environment.

5.6 Public protests and the January 6th Capitol event

Following the 2020 presidential election, there were several public protests and rallies, mostly sparked by worries about purported election fraud and imagined challenges to democratic procedures. On January 6, 2021, a large-scale and violent incident marked the culmination of these protests: a crowd of supporters of then-President Donald Trump stormed the U.S. Capitol in Washington, D.C. This incident turned into a significant turning point in modern American history that affected public opinion, politics, and security in a big way.

5.6.1 Demonstrations in Public

In the wake of the 2020 election, nationwide demonstrations broke out. The main organizers of these protests were Trump supporters who wanted to show their support for Trump's allegations of electoral fraud as well as their dissatisfaction with the election results. The protests ranged in size and intensity from nonviolent get-togethers to confrontational crowds outside of electoral offices and government buildings. A number of well-known rallies and speeches were given in the run-up to January 6. The notion of a rigged election was persistently advanced by Trump and his associates, stoking discontent among his followers. The "Stop the Steal" protests were notable because speakers there echoed claims of electoral fraud and urged people to keep opposing the outcome of the election.

5.6.2   The January 6th Capitol Riot

Congress met on January 6, 2021, to officially ratify the 2020 presidential election's Electoral College results. In front of a sizable gathering of his supporters that morning close to the White House, President Trump restated his accusations of election fraud and exhorted them to "fight like hell." Many of the participants marched to the Capitol after his address. As the mob became aggressive, the situation quickly got out of control. Thousands of Trump fans stormed through security guards, smashed windows, and went into the Capitol. The rioters fought with law enforcement, plundered property, and vandalized offices. There were many fatalities, countless injuries, and significant property damage as a consequence of the assault.

The intrusion resulted in an instant lockdown of the Capitol, forcing Congress to adjourn for a short while. To re-establish order, law police and National Guard personnel were sent. Politicians from all parties, including several Republicans, strongly denounced the incident, citing the violence and interference with the political process as their main grievances.

5.6.3   Repercussions and Aftereffects

A number of people were arrested and prosecuted in the wake of the Capitol riot. Numerous participants faced charges that varied from assaulting law enforcement officials to trespassing. Additional security measures were implemented as a result of the incident in state capitals around the nation as well as in Washington, D.C. The House of Representatives accused President Trump of "incitement of insurrection," which led to his second impeachment. Even though the Senate ultimately cleared Trump, the impeachment was a pivotal point in the continuing political drama surrounding his administration.

The events of January 6th had a significant influence on public discussion, resulting in heightened discussions over political violence, disinformation, and the function of social media. The riot also refocused attention on the duties of elected officials in combating and denouncing radicalism, as well as the influence that political leaders have on public opinion. The Capitol riot has had a lasting impact on American politics, resulting in arguments about democratic standards and election integrity continuing, as well as enhanced monitoring of political discourse. Additionally, it has exacerbated conflict and  polarization in American culture. A major and unsettling era in American history was highlighted by the Capitol incident on January 6, which reflected profound differences and heightened political tensions. It emphasised the erratic character of today's political debate as well as the possible fallout from disinformation and bluster. Discussions on democracy, security, and the function of political leadership in upholding democratic institutions are still influenced by this incident.

Chapter No. 06
Preparing for 2024 Election

"As Aristotle observed, 'Man is by nature a political animal.' The anticipation for the 2024 election reflects humanity's intrinsic drive to engage in the political process, to debate, and to choose leaders who will shape the future."

The political scene was characterised by extreme polarization and scrutiny as the 2024 election drew near. Notwithstanding legal difficulties, Donald Trump continued to have a considerable impact inside the Republican Party by emphasizing economic nationalism and anti-establishment discourse. While negotiating its own set of obstacles, the Democratic Party sought to resolve internal divides and build on policy victories. Social fairness, economic recovery, and election integrity were among the main concerns. To guarantee a competitive campaign and solve critical issues, both parties mobilized by fortifying their alliances, generating money, and interacting with people. A very competitive and high-stakes election was anticipated by the plans and preparations for 2024.

6.1 The State of the Nation

6.1.1 Economic Landscape

The American economy was marked by considerable volatility and change by 2024. The COVID-19 pandemic had a varied effect on various industries and demography, making the recovery from it uneven. For many Americans, inflation rates continued to be a serious issue since they affected their buying power and cost of living. The national conversation revolved on initiatives to address wage growth, job creation, and economic inequities. The recovery experienced varying degrees of success, with some industries picking up steam while others took longer. Infrastructure improvements and government stimulus plans attempted to boost economy, but problems including labour shortages and supply chain disruptions continued. Increasing demand, problems with the supply chain, and growing energy costs all contributed to inflation, which continued to be a serious problem. For many families, the effect on regular spending and savings was a major issue. Although there were indications of progress, issues including mismatched skill sets and the impact of technology persisted in influencing employment patterns. A major topic of discussion was the need for improved working conditions and greater salaries.

6.1.2 Cultural and Social Concerns

Social and cultural problems were crucial in forming the character of the country. Political agendas and public conversation were dominated by issues like climate change, gender equality, and racial justice. Calling for changes and tackling structural injustices, movements promoting social justice and racial equality endured.

These movements had a noticeable influence on public opinion and policy discussions. Discussions on environmental legislation, investments in renewable energy, and climate adaptation techniques persisted, and climate change continued to be a serious concern. Political and corporate actions were impacted by public demand for more aggressive action on climate-related concerns.

Concerns about financing for education and healthcare reform persisted. Ensuring fair educational opportunities, addressing mental health concerns, and enhancing access to affordable healthcare were the main priorities.

6.1.3 The Political Environment

2024 saw a considerable increase in political polarization and agitation. There was distrust and discord as a result of recent political events, such as the Capitol riot on January 6th and continuing investigations. With stark differences between partisan factions on important topics, political polarization increased. This polarization had an impact on public discourse and legislative procedures, often resulting in deadlock and divisive discussions. Activists at the grassroots level were crucial in influencing political agendas and energizing the electorate. Activist organisations influenced public opinion and policy deliberations by focusing on a variety of causes, such as environmental conservation and election integrity.

The public's confidence in the courts, government, and media remained brittle. In order to restore trust and promote a more unified community, efforts to address concerns of accountability, openness, and change were essential.

6.1.4   Global Positioning and Foreign Policy

Key topics of discussion in the country were the foreign policy and worldwide posture of the United States. The nation's perspective on foreign problems has been influenced by commercial ties, geopolitical conflicts, and international alliances. U.S. foreign policy was heavily influenced by ties to major world powers like China and Russia. Diplomatic tactics and international discussions were impacted by issues such as commerce, security, and human rights. The United States' economy and its place in the world economy were significantly shaped by trade agreements and policies. The goals were supply chain vulnerabilities, fair trade practices promotion, and trade deficit balance. The United States persisted in navigating its partnerships and alliances, attempting to fortify ties with important allies while tackling obstacles in global security and diplomacy.

In 2024, the country faced economic difficulties, social and cultural discussions, political division, and intricate worldwide relationships. In order to address these problems and position the nation for a secure and successful future, careful navigation and strategic planning were needed.

6.2   Economic and Social Conditions in 2024

6.2.1   Economic Condition

After the COVID-19 pandemic caused disruptions, the US economy was in a period of recovery in 2024. Although there was development in a number of areas, the rate of recovery differed greatly. While some sectors, like healthcare and technology, recovered quickly, others, including retail and hotels, found it difficult to return to their pre-pandemic levels. A major worry going forward was inflation, which was fuelled by interruptions in the supply chain, growing energy costs, and a rise in the demand for products and services. As a result, regular goods became more expensive, placing pressure on family finances. Through changes to interest rates and other monetary measures, the Federal Reserve and legislators attempted to control inflation. Although the unemployment rate was declining, there were still difficulties in the labour market. There was a skills gap that many workers had to deal with, and businesses like manufacturing and services had trouble filling jobs. Automation and the move towards remote work have also had an impact on employment patterns, with a greater focus on digital skills and flexible work schedules. As income gaps across income groups became increasingly noticeable, wealth inequality remained a serious problem. There have been talks about pay hikes, tax changes, and social safety nets as ways to combat inequality. Economic programs intended to assist middle-class and lower-class families were the subject of ongoing discussion on their fairness and efficacy. There were ups and downs in the housing market, with increasing prices for homes and more demand in many regions. For families with lower incomes and first-time buyers, affordability has become a critical concern. In order to alleviate the housing scarcity and provide access to affordable homes, policymakers looked at many options.

6.2.2 Social Situation

There have been continuous discussions about healthcare reform and access, which has been a primary priority. The main topics of discussion around the country were how to manage the pandemic's effects on public health, increase access to inexpensive healthcare, and treat mental health issues. The environment was further shaped by the emergence of telemedicine services and modifications to healthcare legislation. Movements promoting structural changes and equal rights continued to fuel conversations and legislative measures. Social justice concerns, such as racial equity, gender equality, and LGBTQ+ rights, remained prevalent in public debate. These movements had an influence on societal attitudes and legislative actions.

With talks on raising access to high-quality education, mitigating learning loss from the epidemic, and increasing educational results, education was one of the main areas of attention. Important topics were the use of technology in the classroom and the need of funding for educational institutions and faculty. Stress and isolation brought on by the epidemic made mental health a more pressing concern. Social policy has to prioritise efforts to enhance mental health services, lessen stigma, and provide assistance to those who are struggling with mental health issues.

In order to solve social issues and promote unity, community involvement and civic participation were crucial. Volunteer work, community projects, and grassroots movements all contributed to problem solving and better communities. Environmental problems and climate change remained major concerns. Public policy and consumer behaviour have been influenced by the drive for sustainable practices, investments in renewable energy, and climate adaption plans. Social conversations revolved on environmental advocacy and the effects of climate change on local communities.

The United States' social and economic landscape in 2024 was characterised by continued difficulties, recovery initiatives, and shifting priorities. The nation's path as it dealt with the pandemic's aftermath and became ready for future uncertainty was shaped by the interaction of social and economic challenges. It took extensive plans and cooperative efforts from many sectors and communities to address these issues.

6.3   Trump's Comeback

After his turbulent exit from office and the scandals surrounding the 2020 election, Donald Trump's return to the president signaled a turning point in American politics. His comeback was marked by a revitalized presidential campaign in 2024, propelled by a committed fan base, a solid plan, and a goal to re-establish his agenda and prominence in the country.

6.3.1   Rekindled Political Aspirations

Trump's return started with a concise statement outlining his goals for the United States. While addressing the critiques and difficulties encountered throughout his presidency, Trump aimed to build on his prior achievements by highlighting themes from his first term, such as economic development, national security, and a populist agenda. Trump's ability to recast his story and win over both supporters and indifferent voters was essential to his comeback. He promised to address pressing challenges like immigration reform and economic revitalization while building on his prior successes, such as tax reduction and deregulation. As part of his strategy, Trump made use of social media, media appearances, and rallies to tap into his already-established network of followers. His capacity to energies and mobilize his supporters was essential to his resurgence as a front-runner for the presidency.

6.3.2   Dynamics of Campaigns

Trump used conventional and cutting-edge methods in his campaign plan. His group concentrated on mobilizing the grassroots level, focusing on swing states, and using data-driven tactics to increase support and voter participation. The campaign sought to strengthen core support while assembling a large coalition. In order to contact voters, Trump kept up a strong media presence via the use of both mainstream and alternative media outlets. He used direct interaction with supporters, refuted unfavourable stories, and positioned himself as an advocate of US interests and values as part of his communication approach. There were some difficulties with Trump's return. He was subjected to criticism from the Republican Party, legal disputes, and investigation about his involvement in the events of January 6, 2021. Despite these obstacles, his team made an effort to respond to critiques and provide voters a consistent image.

6.3.3   Important Events and Assistance

The Republican Party's well-known members and organisations provided backing for Trump's resurgence. These recommendations gave his candidacy more legitimacy and served to further establish him as the front-runner. A key component of Trump's comeback plan was his attendance at rallies and public events. These occasions not only boosted his support base but also provided him with a stage on which to address people directly about his goals and ideas. Trump's comeback was greatly aided by fundraising. Political action committees (PACs) and individual contributors both contributed a significant amount to his campaign, which he used to finance outreach, advertising, and campaign operations.

6.3.4   Influence on the Political Environment

With numerous politicians and officials endorsing his programs and language, Trump's return had a significant impact on the GOP's course. His impact on the party's program and election-related tactics. The 2024 election environment was significantly influenced by Trump's capacity to energies people and increase turnout. Both his admirers and detractors were energized by his return, which added to the already intensely competitive and tense political atmosphere. With deep divisions between Trump's supporters and opponents, the attention on his return heightened political polarization. The dynamics of the campaign, media coverage, and public conversation around the election were all impacted by this polarization. Trump's 2024 return to politics was a watershed event in American politics, characterised by a calculated campaign, well-known endorsements, and a passionate fan following. His reappearance in politics changed the GOP's terrain, galvanized supporters, and prepared the way for a much awaited presidential contest. The circumstances surrounding his return to politics highlighted the long-lasting effects of his influence and mirrored larger patterns in American politics.

6.4   Announcing the 2024 candidacy

A pivotal point in American politics was reached when Donald Trump declared his campaign for president in 2024. After his contentious exit from the president and the turbulent aftermath of the 2020 election, it marked a formal return to politics. This declaration ushered in a very contested and competitive election season.

6.4.1 The Announcement Event

Trump purposefully timed his announcement of his candidacy to optimise press coverage and public interest. The venue, which was selected to emphasise the importance of his return to politics, was a prominent one. The location and schedule were chosen to draw in the greatest number of people and have the most effect. During his inaugural address, President Trump reiterated his adherence to the fundamental values and program of his first term. He emphasised important subjects including national security, economic recovery, and a return to traditional conservative principles. He emphasised his accomplishments and future vision in his address, which was tailored to appeal to both his devoted supporters and indecisive voters. **3. Symbolic components: The announcement included symbolic components intended to convey a feeling of continuity and regeneration. Images and words linked the incident to his first term, enhancing his reputation as an innovator and a champion of American principles. The use of well-known catchphrases, visuals, and messages strengthened his appeal and brand.

6.4.2 Public and Media Reaction

Networks and sources covered the news in great detail, including live broadcasts along with analysis and comments. The media's reaction differed, with some publications emphasizing Trump's possible influence on the outcome of the election while others highlighted his detractors and scandals. The campaign's tone and public image were greatly influenced by this coverage.

There was divided response to Trump's declaration of candidacy. While detractors expressed doubts and worries, supporters conveyed excitement and a renewed devotion to his cause. Discussions and debates on the announcement went viral on social media, news websites, and political discussion boards. The political climate was significantly altered by the news. It brought up the 2024 election again and brought attention to Trump's campaign. His reappearance in the race sparked a fierce campaign cycle and affected the tactics and positions of other contenders.

6.4.3   The goals and strategy of the campaign

After the announcement, Trump's team made a number of calculated moves to try to gain traction. This included planning demonstrations, interacting with the press, and rallying supporters. The goal of the campaign was to take advantage of the early enthusiasm and turn it into ongoing support and involvement. Trump's campaign had to deal with the fallout from the 2020 election as well as the complaints and issues from his prior administration. The team created plans to refute unfavourable stories and bolster Trump's reputation as a capable and powerful leader. A key element of Trump's campaign plan was fundraising. In order to raise money, the campaign concentrated on using existing donor networks and mobilizing support at the local level. Establishing a solid staff, creating a campaign infrastructure, and putting data-driven voter outreach tactics into practice were all examples of organisational initiatives.

A crucial turning point in the election cycle was reached when Donald Trump declared his campaign for president in 2024, paving the way for a fiercely contested and high-stakes contest. The public's response, the announcement event, and media attention all emphasised how important his return to politics is. Trump's candidacy would change the political environment and impact the dynamics of the 2024 presidential election as the campaign progressed.

6.5   Campaign strategies and key issues

6.5.1   Campaign Strategies

Trump's campaign approach focused on restating his key points from his prior administration. Among them were pledges to maintain conservative principles, bolster national security, and revive the economy. With an emphasis on populism and patriotism, the campaign aimed to establish Trump as the defender of the American people. To reach voters, Trump's campaign made use of his media acumen by using both conventional and social media channels. A comprehensive digital strategy was used by the campaign, which included internet donations, email marketing, and social media advertisements. One of Trump's greatest advantages was his ability to control media attention, which kept his message at the forefront of the national conversation.

To energies his supporters and show support from the general public, Trump's campaign staged many rallies across the nation. The purpose of these rallies was to demonstrate Trump's capacity to energies large gatherings and get media attention while also building momentum and excitement. In order to win the election, the campaign concentrated on important swing states. Targeted outreach and customised message were used as strategies to contact voters in these states, with a focus on addressing problems and concerns specific to the area.

The Trump campaign made a significant investment in establishing a robust ground game, which included setting up neighbourhood campaign offices, enlisting volunteers, and going door-to-door. The goal of this grassroots strategy was to create a network of supporters and directly contact voters. The campaign devised plans to deal with issues and complaints from Trump's prior administration as well as the 2020 election. This includes addressing concerns about Trump's leadership style, responding to legal and political obstacles, and crafting messaging to refute claims of election fraud.

6.5.2   Important Concerns

Trump's pledge to boost the US economy was a major platform throughout the campaign. Plans to lower taxes, loosen industry regulations, and encourage job growth were among them Trump's campaign emphasised his plans to fortify borders, thwart illegal immigration, and bolster national security measures. The campaign also sought to persuade voters that he could bring prosperity back by highlighting his prior achievements in economic growth. The campaign tackled the continuing effects of the COVID-19 pandemic, stressing Trump's reaction and plans for recovery. It also emphasised on Trump's record in these areas and his dedication to preserving a strong and safe country. This included talks on immunization programs, fiscal stimulus packages, and strategies for a safe reopening of the economy.

Trump's campaign gave election integrity a lot of attention, especially in light of the turmoil surrounding the 2020 election. This included addressing concerns about purported fraud and arguing for modifications to the voting process. Trump's campaign tackled a range of cultural and social problems, such as discussions about gun rights, healthcare, and education. The campaign also sought to reassure supporters and advance measures to guarantee fair elections. Trump's campaign highlighted his administration's accomplishments in negotiating trade deals, fortifying alliances, and taking on international foes in order to position himself as a champion of conservative policies on these issues and as a defender of traditional values. The campaign sought to portray Trump as a formidable global leader. **7. Second Amendment Rights: The campaign emphasised the need of defending gun ownership and opposing attempts to enact more stringent gun control laws. This topic was central to Trump's platform and struck a chord with a large number of his fans.

Trump's campaign pushed for the repeal of the Affordable Care Act (Obama care) and the establishment of a new, more conservative healthcare system. Healthcare reform remained a major concern. The campaign focused on pledges to lower expenses and increase healthcare accessibility.

Trump's 2024 election campaign was distinguished by a deliberate focus on major subjects, media presence, grassroots support, and core messaging. Trump sought to energies his supporters and win over a wide variety of people by concentrating on important issues like election integrity, national security, and economic recovery. The main goals of the campaign were to gain traction and establish a commanding lead in the 2024 presidential contest.

6.6 Media and Political Establishment Response

Intensive Examining and Critiquing: From the beginning of Trump's 2024 campaign, there was a great deal of analysis and criticism in the media. Numerous media sources persisted in closely examining Trump's past administration and current scandals, emphasizing his response to the COVID-19 outbreak, purported legal problems, and policy positions. This critical media often drew attention to Trump's presidential campaign's possible flaws and scandals. The mainstream media consistently portrayed Trump's campaign as contentious and polarizing, reflecting the extreme polarization of the reaction to his candidacy. On the other hand, Trump's campaign was often presented favourable by conservative media, which highlighted his accomplishments and characterised the criticism as unfair or biased. The wider political rift in the nation was reflected in this polarization.

The media often focused on legal and ethical concerns pertaining to Trump, such as pending investigations and litigation. Reports on these issues often presented Trump as possibly being in legal peril and casting doubt on his suitability for administration. This emphasis was meant to highlight the difficulties Trump had and cast doubt on his candidacy. The media emphasised the nation's continued political division, often portraying Trump's campaign as a carryover of the divisive language and strategies from his first administration. His controversial public remarks and campaign rallies were widely covered by the media, who portrayed them as representations of a sharply divided electorate.

The media narrative surrounding Trump's campaign was greatly influenced by social media. Memes and trending postings on social media sites like Facebook, Instagram, and Twitter were used to spread both positive and negative messages about Trump, changing the media landscape in the process. Discussions around purported censorship and election integrity also turned social media into a combat zone.

6.6.1 Establishment Politics' Reaction

Leaders and legislators on the left were outspoken in their opposition to Trump's candidature, focusing on his record during the previous administration and painting him as a danger to democratic principles. The Democratic Party contrasted its leadership and programs with Trump's agenda in an effort to unite people behind a vision of an alternate future. The reaction to Trump's campaign among the Republican establishment was hardly unanimity. While a number of Republican leaders and elected officials remained supportive of Trump, others voiced doubts or critiqued some parts of his campaign. This internal split was a reflection of larger party discussions on the GOP's leadership and course.

A number of political figures—including some Republicans and Democrats—have stressed the need of election reform and integrity. Talks over purported errors and fraud from the 2020 election continued to influence political discourse, with a number of prominent figures demanding voting process reforms and more transparency. During Trump's campaign, the political establishment discussed a number of important topics, including as immigration, healthcare, and economic policies. These talks and conflicts often revolved around divergent policy stances and outlooks for the future of the nation, with Trump's opinions acting as a focal point. Scholars and political figures addressed the ways in which Trump used media and rallies as part of his campaign. While some saw Trump's strategy as successful and appealing to his supporters, others saw it as polarizing or detrimental to the political dialogue. The political spectrum as a whole responded to Trump's campaign tactics in somewhat different ways. Other Republican candidates and leaders' stances and tactics were impacted by Trump's campaign, which had a major effect on party dynamics. The GOP's policies and rhetoric were influenced by his campaign, with some leaders closely identifying with his ideology and others trying to set themselves apart from him.

Trump's 2024 campaign drew strong criticism, polarization, and discussion from the political elite and media. The political establishment was characterised by resistance from Democrats, internal tensions within the GOP, and continuous disputes over election integrity and important policy problems. Meanwhile, media coverage concentrated on the legal, ethical, and contentious elements of Trump's campaign.

Chapter No. 07
The Great Awakening and the Golden Age

"As John Locke emphasized, 'The end of law is not to abolish or restrain, but to preserve and enlarge freedom.' The Great Awakening ushers in an era where individuals awaken to their true potential, leading to a Golden Age of expanded freedom and prosperity."

Some people see the Great Awakening as a revolutionary time when people transcend from the Deep State's manipulative control and awaken to a greater level of awareness and knowledge. This awakening, which is characterised by the revelation of covert goals and the birth of new paradigms that upend established power structures, is seen as a communal realisation of the truth. Believing in the impending Golden Age—a time of unheard-of wealth, freedom, and harmony—is essential to this awakening. This imagined period, which would bring in innovations like Tesla technology, medical beds, and flying automobiles, promises to offer a break from the problems facing society now. Proponents contend that a worldwide movement towards enlightenment will define this Golden Age, and that mankind will have access to technology and information that have long been kept by privileged groups. Those who support the Great Awakening believe that leaders like Trump were crucial in toppling the previous regime and ushering in this new one. They see his presidency as a spark that will bring about the significant adjustments needed to make this optimistic picture of a revitalized world a reality.

7.1 What is the Great Awakening?

Although there are many different ways to understand the term "Great Awakening," it usually refers to a momentous time when people experienced a great change in consciousness and understanding. Here are a few crucial elements:

- **Spiritual and Consciousness Shift:** The phrase often refers to an elevated state of consciousness or enlightenment in which people discover more profound truths about the world, society, and themselves. This change is usually characterised by a rejection of traditional ideologies and thought processes in favor of more spiritual or holistic viewpoints.

- **Historical Context:** Throughout American history, the term "Great Awakening" has been used to describe a number of religious awakenings, including the First Great Awakening (18th century) and the Second Great Awakening (early 19th century). Reform and broad religious fervor characterised these movements.

- **Contemporary Usage:** The term "Great Awakening" refers to a widespread realisation of what some consider to be hidden facts concerning deep state activities, elite control, and global government. This is particularly true among activist or conspiracy theory circles. It often alludes to the discovery of alleged worldwide conspiracies and the emergence of a collective consciousness that aims to overthrow these control mechanisms.

- **Cultural and Social Implications:** The Great Awakening is seen by supporters as the precursor to a new period of human civilization marked by more peace, fairness, and freedom. It is common to imagine radical shifts in technology, government, and social values at this time. Advocates of the Great Awakening saw it as a revolutionary movement that brought about a civilization that was more united, powerful, and enlightened overall.

7.2 Origins and Beliefs of the Great Awakening

Originally used to describe a string of religious revivals in American history, the phrase "Great Awakening" Religious reform and revival were prevalent throughout the First Great Awakening (1730s–1740s) and the Second Great Awakening (early 19th century), which had a profound effect on American society and culture. These groups placed a strong emphasis on intimate relationships with the divine, emotional involvement in worship, and personal piety.

In modern times, the Great Awakening has come to represent a more widespread, worldwide awakening, particularly in certain alternative and conspiracy theory circles. It is seen as an era of enlightenment during which people see and reject alleged deep state players and global elites' hidden goals and manipulations.

7.2.1 Fundamental Principles

- **Knowledge of Hidden Truths:** Proponents of the contemporary Great Awakening contend that influential elite organisations have concealed or distorted certain facts regarding historical events, society systems, and international governance. This covers ideas of international conspiracies, secret societies, and clandestine government activities.

- **Spiritual Enlightenment:** Many people connect the Great Awakening with a spiritual or consciousness change, in which people accept a higher state of awareness and go beyond what is typically understood. This might include a stronger emphasis on one's own spirituality, holistic treatment, and alternate realities.

- **Rejecting the Status Quo:** There is a strong conviction that the current power structures, which are seen as corrupt or repressive, must be challenged and overthrown. Proponents want to create a new global order based on fairness, freedom, and transparency by enacting substantial reforms to the political, economic, and social structures.

- **Vision of a Golden Age:** There is a widespread notion that the Great Awakening will bring in a "Golden Age," which will be marked by unheard-of levels of affluence, scientific achievement, and social peace. This envisions a more educated global society as well as the introduction of cutting-edge technology like free energy and medical beds.

Key personalities' Role: Some people think that specific people, including public personalities or political leaders, are essential in helping to bring about this awakening. People like Donald Trump, for example, are often seen as playing a key role in exposing the deep state and spearheading the transition to a new age of wealth and freedom.

All things considered, the contemporary understanding of the Great Awakening embraces a wide spectrum of religious, political, and social ideologies that are based on the notion of a revolutionary movement towards a society that is more emancipated and enlightened.

7.3   Envisioning the Golden Age

The notion of the Golden Age envisions a utopian future in which civilization reaches a level of unheard-of peace, wealth, and development. This vision often incorporates aspects of technology progress, social transformation, and spiritual enlightenment. This is the conventional conception of the Golden Age:

7.3.1   Technological Progress

The Golden Age is often linked to ground-breaking developments in medicine, such as med beds—machines that can quickly restore and revitalise the body. This includes the elimination of ordinary illnesses and the treatment of disorders that were previously incurable. It is anticipated that technological advancements in energy production, such as free energy systems, would end the need for fossil fuels, lessen their negative effects on the environment, and provide an endless supply of clean energy sources. Cutting-edge innovations that improve everyday life and simplify many facets of civilisation, such as flying automobiles, extremely complex robots, and AI systems, may also be integrated during this age.

7.3.2   Prosperity in both social and economic domains

The vision calls for a sharp rise in economic prosperity, with a particular emphasis on wealth distribution to guarantee that everyone has fair access to opportunities and resources. This is often associated with the substitution of novel, deemed more equitable and transparent models, like cryptocurrencies, for more established financial institutions. The elimination of inequality and poverty is a fundamental feature of the Golden Age. It is widely believed that improved economic systems and cutting-edge technology will enable everyone to live comfortably and reach their full potential. The vision places a strong emphasis on raising living standards, providing access to top-notch education, and providing cutting-edge leisure and recreational opportunities. The focus is on building a society in which individuals may prosper both personally and professionally.

7.3.3   Cultural and Spiritual Awakening

People often see the Golden Age as a period of spiritual enlightenment during which they attained a greater degree of awareness and a stronger connection with their inner selves. This calls for a better comprehension of spiritual concepts and a closer relationship with the cosmos.

Cultural, racial, and national divides are expected to give way to a more accepting and peaceful globe during this period of global unification. Mutual respect, a set of shared values, and objectives unite us. Integrity, compassion, and fairness are valued in all facets of life, and there is a perception of a substantial movement towards higher ethical and moral standards.

7.3.4   Reforms in Politics and Society

The Golden Age is often depicted as a time when repressive institutions and systems are overthrown and individual liberties are completely restored and safeguarded. This entails changes to the legal and governance structures to guarantee more accountability and openness. This fundamental principle enables people to directly impact social decisions and the course of society by empowering both individuals and communities. Advances in governance might result in more decentralised, participatory systems with more equitable power distribution and public participation in decision-making.

7.3.5   A New World's Vision

The Golden Age often emphasises sustainability, with eco-friendly methods and innovations guaranteeing the environment's preservation for coming generations. A strong focus is placed on the creative and cultural aspects of life, with the arts and creativity being essential components of society. This covers the development of artistic expression as well as the honouring of various cultural achievements. All things considered, the Golden Age vision points to a revolutionary age in which mankind overcomes contemporary constraints to reach a condition of peace, wealth, and knowledge.

7.4   Proposed Reforms and Policies for the Golden Age

A number of revolutionary laws and regulations aimed at building a more just, affluent, and enlightened society are part of the Golden Age concept. The following significant changes and policies that are in line with this vision are proposed:

7.4.1   Reforms in the Economy

The goal of the UBI is to guarantee that every person gets a monthly, unconditional payment to meet the necessities of life. This seeks to lower poverty and provide everyone financial stability. To combat income inequality, progressive taxation and wealth redistribution measures are put into place. To pay for social services and infrastructure, this entails raising taxes on companies and the very rich. Using cryptocurrencies, such as XRP and XLM, in place of conventional fiat currencies as new means of payment and financial exchange. The objective is to improve the efficiency and transparency of finance. The advancement of alternative economic models that put the welfare of the community ahead of the pursuit of profit maximisation, such as cooperative corporate structures and decentralised finance (DeFi).

7.4.2   Technological Progress

Using cutting-edge medical equipment, such med beds, to promote recovery quickly and enhance health outcomes. This involves funding the development of public health infrastructure and the hunt for illness remedies. To end dependency on fossil fuels and lessen environmental effect, significant investment is being made in renewable energy sources and technologies, such as solar, wind, and fusion power. The creation of technologically integrated smart cities that maximise urban life. This covers automated waste management, smart transportation systems, and economical energy consumption. More resources and attention are being allocated to space exploration and colonisation with the goal of extending human presence beyond Earth and advancing science.

7.4.3   Policies Concerning Social and Environmental Issues

Tightening environmental laws to safeguard natural resources, halt climate change, and encourage sustainable lifestyles. This covers programs aimed at reducing pollution, conserving animals, and planting new trees. Redesign the curriculum with an emphasis on creativity, critical thinking, and practical skills. As part of this, technological integration and individualised learning programs are used to better prepare pupils for the future. Enacting laws to guarantee that everyone has access to inexpensive housing. This covers assistance for low-income households as well as incentives for the construction of sustainable dwellings. To address concerns of unfairness and inequality, a comprehensive reform of the criminal justice system is necessary. This includes actions to strengthen community policing, lower mass prison rates, and improve rehabilitation programs.

7.4.4   Reforms in Political and Governance

Using decentralised modes of government to strengthen local communities and lessen power concentration. Supporting grassroots movements and inclusive decision-making procedures falls under this category. Putting policies in place to improve accountability and transparency in the public and private sectors. This include measures like open data campaigns, anti-corruption legislation, and improved supervision procedures. To guarantee justice and equality for all people, human rights safeguards should be strengthened. This covers actions to combat prejudice, encourage diversity, and safeguard civil freedoms. Encouraging international collaboration and diplomacy to tackle worldwide issues and promote amicable ties among states. Supporting international accords on security, health, and climate change is part of this.

7.4.5   Improvements in Culture and Spirituality

Funding for cultural endeavours and the arts is allocated to improve artistic expression and cultural enrichment. Support for artists, cultural organisations, and community arts initiatives fall under this category. Through instruction and community initiatives, spiritual and personal development are encouraged. This involves having access to tools for mindfulness, meditation, and overall health. Initiatives to promote respect for one another and diversity while celebrating social cohesiveness and inclusion. This includes programs aimed at bridging socioeconomic, racial, and cultural gaps.

The Golden Age's ideal of a society marked by wealth, equality, and enlightenment is what these suggested changes and policies aim to achieve. The objective is to create a future in which every person may prosper and have a positive impact on the world by tackling important issues

7.5   The role of technology and innovation (Med beds, QFS)

Innovation and technology are essential to reshaping society and raising standards of living in the imagined Golden Age. The Quantum Financial System (QFS) and other significant technology developments like medical beds are essential to this change. Here is a thorough analysis of their functions and effects:

7.5.1   Med Beds

Med beds are a revolutionary development in medical science. These gadgets have the potential to completely transform healthcare and human well-being by enabling quick cellular repair and regeneration

Key Functions and Benefits

- Regenerative Healing: To speed up the healing process for a variety of ailments, medical beds use cutting-edge technology including bioelectronic stimulation and frequency treatment. This include healing chronic illnesses, repairing damaged tissues, and encouraging general health recovery.

- Disease Prevention: Med beds may help prevent illnesses and lessen the need for intrusive treatments by boosting the body's natural healing processes. This change may result in lower healthcare expenses and better public health outcomes.

- Personalised medicine: Med beds provide tailored treatment regimens based on personal health information, enabling more focused and less invasive targeted treatments than those provided by conventional techniques.

- Improved Wellness: Med beds have uses beyond medicine that promote overall health and renewal. They may encourage a better lifestyle by reducing stress, enhancing physical vigour, and improving sleep quality.

Effect on the Community:

- Healthcare Revolution: With an emphasis on preventative and regenerative medicine, the sector may undergo a change as a result of the widespread use of medical beds. This change may lessen the strain on healthcare systems and increase patient access.

- Quality of Life: Med beds improve people's overall quality of life by managing health conditions more effectively and quickly, allowing them to lead healthier and more satisfying lives.

- Economic Implications: Lower insurance premiums and medical expenditures for individuals and families are just a few of the beneficial financial consequences that may result from lower healthcare costs and better health outcomes.

7.5.2 Quantum Financial System (QFS):

A cutting-edge financial system called the Quantum Financial System (QFS) was created to modernise and safeguard international financial operations. It seeks to replace antiquated systems with a framework that is more open, effective, and safe.

Key Features and Benefits

- Enhanced Security: To guarantee the integrity and security of financial transactions, the QFS makes use of blockchain technology and cutting-edge cryptographic techniques. This lowers the possibility of financial crimes, fraud, and hacking.
- Transparency and Accountability: The QFS makes it simpler to monitor and validate financial activity by providing a transparent record of all transactions via the use of distributed ledger technology. This lessens corruption and improves accountability.
- Global Integration: The QFS promotes the efficiency and stability of the world economy by facilitating smooth cross-border transactions and financial integration. It facilitates foreign investment and commerce by supporting a wide range of currencies and financial products.
- Decentralisation: The QFS functions on a decentralised paradigm, empowering people and diminishing the influence of centralised financial institutions, in contrast to conventional financial systems that depend on central authority.

Effect on the Community:

- Economic Stability: By lowering systemic risks and increasing the effectiveness of financial transactions, the QFS may improve global financial stability. This may help to make the world economy more robust and stable.
- Financial Inclusion: The QFS can empower those who are underserved by conventional banking systems and advance financial inclusion by enhancing the accessibility and security of financial services.
- Decrease in Corruption: The QFS's security and transparency characteristics may aid in the fight against illegal activity and financial corruption, promoting a more just and reliable financial environment.
- Innovation and Growth: By encouraging the creation of new financial goods and services, the QFS may stimulate innovation in the financial industry. This might spur economic expansion and open up new doors for people and companies.

According to the Golden Age vision, innovation and technology will play a major role in creating a brighter future. The Quantum Financial System and medical beds are two examples of how cutting-edge technology might solve important problems in healthcare and finance, respectively. These advances help to build a more successful, just, and enlightened society by boosting financial stability, encouraging transparency, and improving health results. Their assimilation into daily existence has the capacity to reshape human experiences and pave the way for a revolutionary period of advancement and prosperity.

7.6   Challenges to the Golden Age

A number of obstacles stand in the way of society's aspirations for a Golden Age marked by wealth, health, and innovation. To fully realise the promise of this revolutionary period, it is imperative that these difficulties be addressed. The following are some of the main challenges that might affect the path to the Golden Age:

7.6.1   Resistance from Established Interests

Power structures and established interests that stand to gain from the current quo may oppose the shift to a Golden Age. These organisations could try to obstruct advancement in order to maintain their power and influence.

Principal Difficulties:

- Economic Disruption: Businesses and industries that face competition from emerging ideas and technology, including QFS and med beds, may oppose change in order to maintain their market share. This may result in attempts to impede or stop developments via lobbying, court cases, and disinformation efforts.
- Political Opposition: Institutions and political leaders having a stake in preserving the status quo in power may be against reforms and changes that might lessen their clout or influence. Both popular opposition and legislative impediments are examples of this resistance.
- Public Scepticism: People may be leery of new technology and systems due to ingrained attitudes and customs. Gaining the public's confidence and overcoming scepticism are crucial for broad adoption.

7.6.2 Risks Related to Technology and Security

There are hazards and possibilities associated with the fast evolution of technology. To avoid any problems, it is essential to guarantee the security and dependability of modern technologies like the QFS and medical beds.

Principal Difficulties:

- Cybersecurity Risks: With the advancement of financial and medical technology, there is an increased risk of cyberattacks. It is crucial to guarantee that these systems are secure against hackers and data breaches.
- Technology Reliability: To make sure new technologies are reliable and safe, they must go through a thorough testing and validation process. Any flaws or faults in med bed systems have the potential to erode effectiveness and confidence.
- Ethical Issues: Using cutting-edge technology brings up ethical issues, especially with respect to permission, privacy, and the fair sharing of advantages. Resolving these issues is essential to preserving public trust.

7.6.3 Gaps in Socioeconomic Status

There may be differences in access and opportunity as a result of the Golden Age's advantages not being spread fairly. It is essential to tackle socioeconomic disparities to guarantee that progress serves everybody.

Main Difficulties

- Access to Technology: Initially, only some populations or geographic areas may have access to advanced technology such as med beds and the QFS. It is essential to provide affordable and universal access in order to avoid creating a gap between various socioeconomic groups.

- Economic Inequality: If a new economic system is not implemented with adequate management, current inequities may become worse. It is necessary to make an effort to guarantee that the advantages of the Golden Age are dispersed equally.
- employment Displacement: Traditional sectors may see employment losses as a result of the adoption of new technology. It is essential to provide assistance and reeducation to impacted labourers in order to alleviate adverse economic consequences.

7.6.4   Tensions in Geopolitics

Geopolitical tensions and wars may have an impact on global progress. To overcome these obstacles, international collaboration and diplomacy are needed.

Principal Difficulties:

- International Relations: Geopolitical rivalries and conflicts may emerge with the adoption of new technology and financial systems. For the world to remain stable, trade conflicts must be avoided and international cooperation must be guaranteed.
- Regulatory Differences: Standards and laws pertaining to developing technology may differ across nations. For innovations to succeed, these standards must be harmonised and worldwide compatibility must be guaranteed.
- International Coordination: Several nations and financial institutions must work together in order for international systems like the QFS to be implemented effectively. Reaching an understanding and working together might be difficult.

7.6.5 Ideological and Cultural Barriers

The adoption and assimilation of new technology and reforms may be influenced by cultural and ideological disparities. Overcoming these obstacles is essential to a seamless transition into the Golden Age.

Principal Difficulties

- Cultural Resistance: The perception of new policies and technology may be shaped by cultural values and customs. Respecting cultural differences and interacting with communities are essential for a successful implementation.
- Ideological Conflicts: Opposition to change may result from opposing ideologies and viewpoints on the place of government and technology. Fostering communication and comprehension may aid in bridging these gaps.
- Education and Awareness: Overcoming opposition and promoting acceptance need that people be aware of the advantages and disadvantages of new technology.

There are several obstacles in the way of the Golden Age, including existing interests' opposition, technology and security dangers, socioeconomic divides, geopolitical conflicts, and cultural hurdles. A holistic strategy that incorporates strong security measures, fair benefit distribution, diplomatic initiatives, and cultural sensitivity is needed to overcome these challenges. Society may strive towards achieving the goal of a Golden Age characterised by wealth, health, and creativity for all by skilfully navigating these obstacles.

7.7   Opposition from the Deep State

The term "Deep State" describes a covert web of people and organisations in the armed forces, intelligence services, and other influential organisations that are said to function independently of elected authorities and have a big say in how policies and decisions are made. The Deep State's hostility may provide significant obstacles to the Golden Age goal. An outline of this resistance and its ramifications is provided below:

7.7.1   Nature of Deep State Opposition

It is believed that the Deep State works in the background to preserve the status quo and opposes any reforms that will undermine its power. This resistance may take many forms, such as clandestine operations, political manoeuvring, and information gathering.

Important Elements:

- Opposition to Reforms: The Deep State may be against Golden Age-era programs and reforms, such as new economic structures or technological advancements, since these might compromise their power and sway.
- Undermining Initiatives: Misinformation, regulatory barriers, and other strategies meant to impede advancement may undermine attempts to advance new laws or technology.
- Influence Operations: To decrease support for suggested reforms and forward its own goal, the Deep State may use its resources to sway public opinion and foment conflict.

7.7.2 The Deep State's techniques

It is thought that the Deep State uses a variety of techniques to thwart movements and laws that pose a danger to its authority. To properly handle their influence, it is vital to comprehend these techniques.

Key Strategies:

- Media Manipulation: The Deep State may manipulate narratives and disseminate false information by controlling media outlets. Confusion, scepticism, and a decline in public support for new efforts might result from this.
- Political subversion: It is possible to stop the implementation of important changes by persuading political institutions and leaders to reject or obstruct reforms. This might include political endorsements, surreptitious pressure, or lobbying.
- Economic Disruption: To obstruct new laws or technological advancements that pose a danger to the Deep State's goals, the State may use economic strategies like financial instability or market manipulation.
- information operations: By monitoring, undermining, or discrediting influential change advocates, covert acts and information collection may be employed to reduce their efficacy and impact.

7.7.3 Effect on the Golden Age Vision

The Deep State's opposition may have a significant impact on the Golden Age's ability to come to pass. This resistance has the power to obstruct development, create barriers, and affect public opinion.

Key Strategies:

- Delayed Implementation: Opposition tactics may cause delays in the implementation of new policies and technology, delaying the Golden Age vision's advancement.

- popular Distrust: It may be difficult to get widespread support for new ideas and leaders when there is popular mistrust due to media manipulation and disinformation tactics.

- Political gridlock: Opposition and political subversion may cause parliamentary deadlock and gridlock, which hinders the adoption of crucial changes and programs.

- Economic Uncertainty: When new systems and technologies are seen negatively, it may lead to resistance and uncertainty among organisations and people.

7.7.4   Countering Deep State resistance

Overcoming Deep State resistance requires a multipronged strategy that includes openness, participation from the public, and calculated countermeasures.

Important Strategies:

- Encourage openness: Promoting openness in policy and decision-making procedures may aid in fostering public confidence and thwarting false information.

- Strengthen Institutions: Reforms and technological advancements may be supported by creating robust institutions that are less vulnerable to Deep State control.

- Encourage Public Engagement: By educating and conversing with the public, new projects may gain support and refute false information.

- Make Use of Alternative Media: You may lessen the effect of the Deep State by using alternative media outlets to combat biassed narratives and provide factual facts.

- Legal and Political Action: Challenging excessive influence and guaranteeing accountability via legal and political means may aid in countering the Deep State's strategies.

The Deep State's opposition poses serious obstacles to realising the Golden Age goal. This resistance may manifest itself in a number of ways, such as economic disruption, political subversion, and media manipulation. To effectively combat this resistance, openness, robust institutions, public participation, and the tactical use of alternative media are necessary. Despite the barriers provided by vested interests, the Golden Age vision may be achieved by taking proactive measures to overcome these issues.

7.8   Potential Conflicts and Solutions

7.8.1   Political Gridlock and Resistance Conflict

Political gridlock is the result of rival groups unable to come to a consensus on important changes or policies, often as a result of entrenched interests or Deep State involvement. This opposition has the potential to impede the Golden Age's progress and stall important projects.

Resolutions:

- Bipartisan Efforts: Create alliances across political lines in order to promote bipartisan collaboration. In order to establish common ground and speed the approval of significant changes, engage with moderate voices from both sides.

- Grassroots Mobilisation: To garner widespread public support, fortify grassroots movements. Legislators may be swayed by popular pressure, which also provides impetus for change.

- Strategic Compromise: To advance while considering the concerns of opposing groups, strive for concessions and small, gradual reforms. This strategy may aid in breaking through deadlock and promote incremental progress.

7.8.2 Media Manipulation and Misinformation

Misinformation and media manipulation have the power to skew public opinion and erode support for novel laws or technological advancements. Because of the Deep State's influence over conventional media, misinformation and misunderstanding may be propagated.

Solutions:

- Alternative Media: Support and encourage media outlets that provide factual and impartial reporting. To combat slanted narratives, support citizen reporting and independent journalism.

- Media Literacy: Fund media literacy initiatives to assist the general public in assessing news sources critically and differentiating between accurate and false information.

- Transparent Communication: Make sure there is transparency in communication by giving the public easy access to understandable, fact-based information. To dispel myths and clear up confusion, using recognised avenues and forums.

7.8.3 Economic Disruption and Instability

Financial instability or market manipulation are two examples of economic disruptions that may erode trust in innovative technology and systems. These strategies might be used by the Deep State to obstruct and oppose reform initiatives.

Solutions:

- Increasing Economic Resilience: Put policies in place that strengthen economic resilience and lessen susceptibility to manipulation. To lessen the effects of disruptions, encourage stability and diversity in important industries.

- Regulatory monitoring: To keep an eye out for and handle any possible market manipulation or economic instability, bolster regulatory monitoring. Make sure there is accountability and transparency in financial systems.

- Public trust: By addressing concerns and showcasing the advantages of new economic systems, increase public trust in them. Give people and companies the information and assistance they need to adjust to change.

7.8.4 Public Mistrust and Division

Deep State resistance may exacerbate public mistrust and division, which makes it difficult to forge broad support for the Golden Age idea. Media bias, political scheming, and disinformation may make these problems worse.

Resolutions:

- Unified Messaging: Create a succinct, unified message that highlights the advantages of suggested changes and responds to public concerns. To reach a large audience, use a variety of communication methods.

- Community Engagement: Get involved in local communities to build trust and solve issues that are specific to them. Encourage communication and teamwork to heal rifts and advance understanding.

- Accountability and Transparency: Make sure decision-making procedures are accountable and open. Show your dedication to moral behaviour and resolve any issues with prejudice or corruption.

7.8.5   Difficulties in the Law and Politics

Conflict: Legal and political issues, such litigation or legislative roadblocks, may obstruct development and cause reform initiatives to fail. The Deep State could obstruct or postpone projects via legal means.

Resolutions:

- Legal Advocacy: Make an investment in this field and provide your support to groups that uphold accountability and justice. Take legal action to stop unjust practices and defend improvements.

- Legislative Strategy: Create a well-thought-out legislative strategy to overcome obstacles and get support for important projects. Collaborate with legal specialists and legislators to overcome any roadblocks.

- Public Advocacy: Encourage the public to support political and legal initiatives. To increase awareness and create pressure for change, use advocacy campaigns and neighbourhood initiatives.

Deep State resistance calls for a multipronged strategy that incorporates community participation, media engagement, political strategy, and economic resilience to effectively address the possible conflicts that may arise. Overcoming entrenched interests and moving closer to the Golden Age ideal may be accomplished by proactively addressing these issues and putting good solutions in place. Despite the obstacles encountered, advancement is possible via cooperation, openness, and calculated action.

CHAPTER NO. 08
RETRIBUTION AND JUSTICE

"As Edmund Burke insightfully remarked, 'The only thing necessary for the triumph of evil is for good men to do nothing.' The quest for retribution and justice reflects the collective resolve to confront and dismantle malevolence, ensuring a righteous path forward."

The goals of Justice and Retribution are to right the wrongs committed by the Deep State and rebuild trust. Retribution aims to hold people accountable for unlawful actions by punishing those who engage in misbehaviour and corruption. Justice includes more comprehensive initiatives to address underlying problems, rebuild public confidence, and advance just government. This include enforcing accountability on the part of people and organisations, guaranteeing openness in enquiries and legal proceedings, and putting changes in place to deal with underlying problems. The ultimate goals of justice and revenge are to topple corrupt institutions and create a more fair and reliable society going forward.

8.1 Lawfare and Legal Battles

Lawfare is the tactical use of legal procedures and institutions to accomplish political or strategic goals; it often entails weaponising or using the law to weaken adversaries. Lawfare has emerged as a key instrument in the struggle between political groups in recent years, especially when it comes to attempts to neutralise, undermine, or discredit political personalities and movements.

Essential Lawfare Aspects:

- Legal Manipulation: Using court cases and legal processes to obstruct, slow down, or harm people's reputations. This involves bringing a lot of baseless cases in an attempt to deplete resources.
- Weaponization of Legal Systems: Using the legal system to further political goals; examples include influencing public opinion and policy results via investigations and prosecutions.
- Strategic Litigation: Using the legal system to accomplish more general strategic objectives, such undermining a political rival or deflecting public attention, rather than necessarily winning a lawsuit.

Lawfare Examples:

- Investigations and Impeachments: When used to politically harm opponents, high-profile investigations and impeachments may be considered Lawfare. It is possible to use these procedures to sow discord and disagreement over the long run.
- Judicial Appointments: Critical case decisions and the legal landscape may be influenced by the deliberate appointment of judges who share certain political or ideological viewpoints.

- Legal challenges to policies: Using legal challenges to thwart or impede legislative and reform agendas as well as policy efforts.

Effects & Repercussions:

- Lawfare contributes to political polarisation by framing legal battles as ideological conflicts, further dividing public opinion.
- Erosion of Trust: Persistent use of Lawfare can undermine public confidence in the legal system, leading to perceptions of bias and corruption.
- Drain of Resources: Litigation may be expensive and resource-intensive, which may cause attention to be drawn away from important problems and policies.

8.1.1 Addressing Lawfare

- Reform: Pushing for judicial and legislative changes to guarantee justice and stop systemic abuse.
- Transparency: To foster accountability and public confidence, legal procedures should be made more transparent.
- Strategic Defence: creating plans to offset law enforcement techniques, such as strong legal defences and public relations campaigns.
- Lawfare continues to be a major obstacle in today's political and legal environments, affecting the sense of justice and the efficiency of government.

8.2 Key legal battles faced by Trump and his allies

8.2.1 Special Counsel Investigations

The Special Counsel Robert Mueller inquiry, which was launched in 2017, looked into possible coordination between the Trump campaign and Russian election meddling. Mueller's report identified many possible cases of obstruction of justice, even if it did not prove collusion. A number of investigations that focused on issues such as the Ukraine controversy ensued, eventually culminating to Trump's impeachment.

8.2.2 Impeachment Procedures

- **First Impeachment (2019–2020):** The House of Representatives convicted Trump of abusing his authority and obstructing Congress in connection with his interactions with Ukraine. Early in 2020, the Senate found him not guilty.
- **Second Impeachment (2021):** Following the Capitol riot on January 6, the House again impeached Trump on allegations of inciting an uprising. Once again, the Senate found him not guilty.

8.2.3 Civil and Criminal Investigations

Manhattan District Attorney's inquiry: Under the direction of Manhattan District Attorney Alvin Bragg, this inquiry looked at possible financial offences, including claims that the Trump Organisation had engaged in financial fraud and tax evasion. New York Attorney General's Investigation: Letitia James, the attorney general of New York, launched a civil probe to find out whether the Trump Organisation had inflated asset values in order to commit fraud.

8.2.4 Legal Challenges and Lawsuits

- **Defamation Lawsuits:** Individuals and organisations filed many defamation lawsuits against Trump and his associates, citing his comments on the 2020 election and other public statements among other things.
- **Lawsuits Concerning the 2020 Election**: Trump and his campaign filed many lawsuits contesting the outcome and conduct of the election. The majority of the time, these lawsuits failed to change the election outcomes.

8.2.5 Opposition to Congressional Subpoenas

Trump and his allies were the subject of congressional subpoenas for a number of enquiries, including those concerning the administration's response to the epidemic and the riot on 6th January. Legal disputes about compliance and executive privilege often resulted from these subpoenas.

8.2.6 Business and Tax Disputes

Tax Disputes involving the Trump Organisation: The Trump Organisation was under investigation for its tax policies, with claims of aggressive tax evasion and inappropriate deductions being made. Public enquiries and continuing legal battles resulted from this attention.

8.2.7 The Capitol violence on January 6th

Legal Actions and Investigations: The Capitol Riot sparked investigations into Trump's involvement and incitement as well as protracted legal processes against those who participated in the violence. Legal disputes over Trump's liability and the wider effects of the incident are still ongoing.

8.2.8   Mar-a-Lago Documents Case

Classified Documents Investigation: There has been a lot of legal scrutiny and the possibility of charges stemming from an investigation into Trump's handling of classified documents, which includes claims that he improperly retained and mishandled sensitive materials at his Mar-a-Lago estate. These court fights are a reflection of the intricate and sometimes acrimonious legal challenges that Trump and his associates have to contend with. These challenges cover a wide variety of topics, from political activities and policy to personal behaviour.

8.3   Martial Law and Military Courts

8.3.1   Military Tribunals

The military formed military tribunals as legal entities to trial people for war crimes or for breaking military law. They have been used in the past to crimes that are not handled by civilian courts or in times of armed conflict. Some have hypothesised that military courts may be utilised to handle claims of treason, corruption, and deep state activity in the context of contemporary discussions and conspiracy theories. These conjectures often stem from worries about alleged overreach by the government and legal responsibility. There are significant legal and constitutional issues surrounding the use of military courts in domestic disputes. There may be a contradiction between the use of military courts for domestic matters and the U.S.

Constitution's provisions of a jury trial and civilian judicial supervision.

8.3.2   Martial Law

This refers to the temporary suspension of civil law and the establishment of military rule over non-combat matters. It is usually proclaimed in the event of extreme situations when regular legal procedures are seen to be inadequate, such as widespread unrest or natural catastrophes.

The proclamation of martial rule would give military authorities the power to impose restrictions on civil freedoms, assume authority over law enforcement, and supersede civilian political systems. It is considered a serious violation of civil rights and is only used as a last option.

Martial rule has been suggested as a possible reaction to political crises such disputed elections or widespread unrest, according to a number of hypotheses and assertions. These accusations are often motivated by worries about possible efforts to stifle dissent or subvert democratic procedures. Proving the inadequacy of standard law enforcement methods is simply one of the many legal and political arguments needed to establish martial rule. The main issues with martial rule are the possibility of power abuse and the effect on civil freedoms.

8.3.3   Accusations and Theories of Conspiracy

According to certain hypotheses, martial rule and military courts might be employed as instruments to deal with purported deep state activity or to thwart attempts by political rivals. These ideas often conjecture about clandestine activities and secret motives. The public's response to these ideas varies; some voice worries about possible overreach, while others support drastic measures to counter perceived dangers. Martial law and military courts are hot topics that can spark heated debates shaped by larger political themes.

8.3.4 Practical Evaluations

In reality, the United States' deployment of martial rule and military courts is governed by strict legal guidelines and control. Adherence to constitutional principles and a convincing reason would be necessary for the adoption of such measures. In the past, martial rule and military courts have seldom been used in the United States and have usually only happened in dire situations, like the American Civil War or World War II. Significant political and legal obstacles would stand in the way of modern applications. Concerns about civil rights, the possibility for abuse, and the authority of the government are still present in the debates surrounding martial rule and military courts. Although these ideas are ingrained in historical and legal frameworks, there is ongoing discussion and controversy around their applicability in modern political environments.

8.4 Historical precedents

8.4.1 Military Courts

Civil War Era

Lincoln Assassination Conspirators Case (1865): Following President Abraham Lincoln's murder, a military court was constituted to prosecute the conspirators, which included co-conspirators John

Wilkes Booth. President Andrew Johnson established this tribunal, and because of the seriousness of the offences and the continuing battles of the Civil War, a military court presided over the proceedings. Ex Parte Milligan (1866): This military trial case set a key judicial precedent. A military tribunal prosecuted Lambdin P. Milligan for his support of the Confederate cause in Indiana. The boundaries of military jurisdiction were upheld when the U.S. Supreme Court declared that it was unlawful to prosecute civilians in military tribunals while civilian courts were in session.

World War II:

Nuremberg Trials (1945–1946): Following the war, the Allies set up military courts at Nuremberg, Germany, to try well-known Nazi officials for crimes against humanity and war crimes. These cases helped to define the fundamentals of responsibility for war crimes, which had a profound impact on the evolution of international law. The Tokyo Trials (1946–1948): The International Military Tribunal for the Far East (IMTFE), which was established to try Japanese war criminals, was modelled after the Nuremberg Trials. Members of the Japanese military and administration were found liable by the trial for crimes against humanity and other wartime atrocities. 8.4.2   Martial Law

American Civil War Era:

Suspension of Habeas Corpus (1861): President Abraham Lincoln permitted the arrest of people without formal charges in certain circumstances during the American Civil War by suspending the writ of habeas corpus. In the midst of a revolt, this action was taken to keep the peace and suppress opposition. The suspension was contentious and was contested in court, most notably in the Ex Parte Merryman case (1861), in which a Maryland citizen opposed the suspension.

World War II

Japanese American Internment (1942): President Franklin D. Roosevelt approved the internment of Japanese Americans in camps all around the country in the wake of the assault on Pearl Harbour. Executive Order 9066 allowed for this action, which was described as a wartime precaution against sabotage and espionage. After the incarceration was publicly denounced and shown to be unfair, the impacted parties received official apologies and compensation.

The Post-9/11 Era

In reaction to the War on Terror, the United States enacted the Military Commissions Act (2006). The Military Commissions Act, approved by Congress, set the process for putting prisoners in Guantanamo Bay and other sites on trial. The purpose of this legislation was to provide a framework for military tribunals conducted outside of the regular civilian legal system and to handle the legal status of enemy combatants.

8.4.3   Contemporary Setting

Constitutional Limitations and Domestic Use

Due to constitutional guarantees, the use of martial rule and military courts in domestic settings is still severely restricted. The extent and implementation of these measures in non-conflict or peacetime situations are constrained by the U.S. Constitution's provisions for the separation of powers and civilian control of military operations.

Legal and Political Difficulties

There would be substantial legal and political obstacles to any effort to impose martial rule or military tribunals in the current political climate in the United States. Such actions might face high judicial and public scrutiny, need a strong reason, and conform to constitutional standards. These historical examples highlight the difficulties and restrictions related to martial rule and military courts in the United States. Although these actions have been taken in dire situations, their use is limited by strict legal requirements and constitutional restrictions.

8.5   Theories and implications for modern times

8.5.1   Theories of Martial Law and Military Tribunals in the Present Context

Necessity Theories

Supporters contend that in dire circumstances when public order is seriously disturbed or national security is in jeopardy, military tribunals and martial rule may be required. They argue that these steps may be necessary to address dangers that are greater than what civilian courts and law enforcement organisations can handle. In order to support the use of exceptional legal frameworks in modern situations, advocates may make comparisons with historical precedents, such as wartime measures or crisis responses. They propose that conclusions from previous crises might guide choices made now.

Issues and Rebuttals:

Opponents claim that martial rule and military courts might jeopardise civil and constitutional liberty. They contend that these actions may breach due process, habeas corpus, and other basic rights, citing past abuses as support. The possibility of power misuse is a source of worry. Critics caution that the imposition of martial rule or military courts may result in arbitrary detentions, political persecution, or a deterioration of democratic standards.

8.5.2   Consequences for the Present Period

Strict judicial review will be applied to any martial law or military tribunal implementation. Such actions would probably be closely examined by courts to make sure they adhere to the law and constitutional safeguards. Cases such as Ex Parte Merryman and Ex Parte Milligan established precedents that influenced judicial judgements and interpretations. Implementing these policies would lead to a heated discussion in both forums. One of the main points of contention would be how to strike a balance between civil freedoms and security, with strong views on both sides. The political climate and the public's confidence in government institutions may be affected by this discussion.

Effects on Civil Rights

If martial law or military tribunals are implemented without appropriate management, civil freedoms may be lost. Concerns pertaining to incarceration without charge or trial, restricted availability to legal counsel, and insufficient openness may emerge, impacting the liberties and rights of people. There may be significant division in the public's view of these actions. While some could consider them an overreach and a danger to democratic norms, others might regard them as essential for maintaining national security. This division may have an impact on popular support for governmental initiatives and election results.

National and International Consequences

The imposition of martial rule and military courts may have an effect on the United States' reputation abroad. These actions may be examined or criticised by foreign friends and organisations, which might have an impact on diplomatic ties and how the world views American government. The military, law enforcement, and judiciary are just a few of the domestic institutions that may be strained by the execution of these policies. Ensuring that measures are both legally sound and successful would need coordination and integration amongst various entities.

Impact of Technology and Information

The implementation and oversight of martial law and military courts may be impacted by the development of digital technology and its surveillance capabilities. Concerns about data security and privacy would be crucial as they might affect the way the data is gathered and used.

The media's role in disseminating information and influencing public opinion are critical in determining how the public will react to these actions. Propaganda and false information have the power to influence people's beliefs and behaviours, which emphasises the need of truthfulness and open reporting. The implementation of martial rule and military courts in the contemporary period would be intricate and multidimensional, incorporating social, political, and legal factors. A major issue would be striking a balance between civil freedoms and national security, with consequences that would affect both the domestic and foreign arenas.

8.6 Judgment Day

8.6.1 Conceptual Understanding

"Judgement Day" is a term used to describe a culmination point in many belief systems when a last evaluation or reckoning takes place. It is connected to heavenly judgement and the ultimate destiny of people or civilisations according to their beliefs and behaviours in religious settings. In a secular or political setting, judgement day may allusively signify a pivotal moment when the results of choices, deeds, or policies are assessed and, often, major adjustments or resolutions are made.

8.6.2 Philosophical Consequences

Spiritual Explanations

According to Christian eschatology, God will judge the souls of the dead on Judgement Day, also known as the Day of Judgement, and will decide their everlasting fate based on their faith and actions. The Book of Revelation and other biblical writings tell of this occurrence. According to Islamic custom, all people are judged by Allah on Judgement Day (Yawm al-Qiyamah), when they are raised from the dead and receive either reward or punishment in the hereafter. A great deal of other faiths also have ideas about the ultimate reckoning or judgement, each with its own meanings and interpretations.

Interpretations that are Secular and Political

In political settings, Judgement Day may represent a point in time when the results of political actions—be they legislative, executive, or otherwise—are completely understood and evaluated. Significant repercussions like government changes, changes in policy, or social upheavals might result from it. It may also refer to the settlement of a significant crisis or conflict, whereby the lessons and long-term impacts are assessed and discussed.

8.6.3   Current Significance and Consequences

Social and Political Impact

In a political or social context, judgement day often has to do with taking responsibility for one's choices and deeds. It entails assessing the efficacy, morality, and influence of leaders and policies, with the aim of producing possible outcomes like changes in leadership, legal action, or reforms.

The idea has the power to shape attitudes and actions of the general public, inspiring demands for justice, reform, or change. It may also act as a focal point for movements aiming to resolve complaints or right perceived wrongs.

Consequences for Law and Institutions

Judgement Day may allude to important court cases or investigations that establish who is responsible for what, particularly where there has been serious legal misconduct, corruption, or abuse of authority. In the event of a judgement day, institutions can see considerable alterations or reforms aimed at resolving systemic problems and bringing about the adoption of measures to re-establish public confidence and efficacy.

Informational and technological influence

Media and communication technologies have a significant impact on how a judgement day situation is portrayed and covered. Public narratives, debates, and the broadcast of information all have a significant impact on how people see the world and react to it. In contemporary settings, technology and digital evidence may be very important in assessing and resolving important problems, which can have an impact on the results of legal, political, or social reckonings.

8.6.4   Cultural and Symbolic Significance

Judgement Day is often used as a potent symbol in discourse and culture, signifying the final conclusion of disputes, the pinnacle of endeavours, or the appraisal of deeds and choices. The idea may emphasise shared goals for fairness, responsibility, and change while also reflecting larger social values and concerns. Judgement Day is essentially interpreted and carries with it a variety of ramifications, ranging from political and social to eschatological and theological. Its importance stems from the deep reflection and closure it embodies, impacting many facets of the human condition and the evolution of society.

8.7   A vision of justice and responsibility

The fundamental tenets of justice and accountability support the operation of institutions, governments, and society. They stand for principles that prioritise justice, openness, and the fair implementation of rules and laws. Providing insights into how these ideals might be realised and sustained, this vision of accountability and justice examines their conceptual underpinning, practical ramifications, and problems in several circumstances.

8.7.1   The Idea of Responsibility

Meaning and Significance

The term "accountability" describes the duty placed on people, groups, or governments to answer to the people they have an impact on about their choices and actions and to take responsibility for their behaviour. It entails a check-and-balances mechanism wherein decisions are scrutinised and repercussions are meted out when obligations are not fulfilled.

Accountability Types

Public workers and elected officials answer to the voters and are required to provide justification for their choices and actions. Through procedures like elections, legislative scrutiny, and public discourse, this accountability is made guaranteed of. Officials and government organisations are required to follow rules, guidelines, and moral principles. Internal controls, audits, and oversight committees uphold administrative accountability.

Corporate Accountability

The public, workers, and shareholders are the parties to whom businesses and companies are responsible. Adherence to legal and regulatory requirements, ethical conduct, and open reporting are all components of corporate responsibility.

Individual Accountability

People are responsible for their acts, especially those in positions of authority or responsibility. This kind of accountability places a strong emphasis on moral conduct and individual accountability.

8.7.2   Accountability-Providing Mechanisms

Openness

Having access to information and decision-making procedures enables interested parties to keep an eye on activities and hold individuals in positions of authority responsible. Transparency averts corruption and promotes confidence.

Oversight Bodies

Independent organisations that monitor and assess the actions of public and commercial enterprises include ombudsmen, auditing firms, and regulatory bodies.

Legal Frameworks

Laws and regulations offer procedures for redress and enforcement in addition to establishing accountability requirements. Laws that prohibit corruption, rules governing conflicts of interest, and safeguards for whistleblowers are examples of legal frameworks.

Public Participation

By embracing many viewpoints and making sure that choices reflect the interests and concerns of impacted communities, including the public in decision-making processes and policy formation improves accountability.

8.8 The Idea of Justice

8.8.1 Meaning and Significance

When someone is treated fairly and their wants and rights are met, they are acting in accordance with the morally righteous and fair notion of justice. It includes procedural justice (fairness in procedures and decision-making) as well as distributive justice (just distribution of resources).

8.8.2 Different Forms of Justice

Emphasises the fair allocation of advantages, opportunities, and resources. It covers topics including social welfare, healthcare and education access, and economic inequality.

Guarantees the fairness, consistency, and transparency of the procedures and methodologies used in decision-making. It highlights the significance of impartiality, due process, and the right to a fair trial. includes enforcing legal sanctions and punishing wrongdoers. It aims to bring the judicial system back into balance and make people responsible for their deeds.

Restorative justice: seeks to make amends and provide reparations in order to heal the damage that criminal activity has caused. In order to remedy the effects of wrongdoing, victims, offenders, and the community must all participate.

8.8.3   Justice Principles

Ensuring that everyone has access to the same opportunities and rights by treating them fairly and without prejudice. Ensuring procedures are transparent and consistent by basing choices on unbiased, objective standards. ensuring that reactions to misconduct are commensurate with the gravity of the transgression, striking a balance between rehabilitation and restitution in addition to punishment.

8.9   Applying Justice and Accountability

Respecting the rule of law guarantees that everyone is subject to the same laws and that they are all implemented equally and consistently. It provides a foundation for legal recourse and enforcement, making it essential to accountability and justice. The enforcement of the law and the fair and impartial resolution of disputes rely on an independent court. It guarantees that judgements on the law are based solely on the facts and the law, unaffected by other forces or influences. Specialised organisations that regulate adherence to legal requirements, look into misbehaviour, and enforce accountability include anti-corruption commissions, human rights organisations, and environmental regulators.

8.8.1   Encouraging Openness and Information Access

Laws that ensure public information is accessible to the public enable people to engage in government and hold public authorities responsible. To foster trust and thwart corruption, government operations, financial reporting, and decision-making procedures must be transparent. Information needed by stakeholders to evaluate performance and accountability is provided by regular reporting on company practices, financial transactions, and government actions. Open disclosures support accountability and openness. Examples of this include yearly reports and audit results.

8.8.2 Promoting Civic Engagement and Public Participation

Including the public in policy development, decision-making procedures, and monitoring tasks guarantees that a range of viewpoints are taken into account and that choices take impacted communities' needs and concerns into account. By bringing attention to issues, enlisting the public's support, and pushing for legislative reforms, civil society organisations, advocacy groups, and grassroots movements are essential in advancing justice and accountability.

8.9 Obstacles & Difficulties

Through the distortion of decision-making processes, the diversion of resources, and the erosion of public confidence, corruption threatens justice and accountability. Comprehensive approaches are needed to combat corruption, such as strong legal systems, efficient enforcement, and an honest and open society.

8.9.1 Discrimination and Inequality

Discrimination and systemic injustices may make it more difficult to administer justice fairly and to hold people accountable. Targeted initiatives to promote inclusion, equitable opportunity, and just treatment for all people are necessary to address these problems.

8.9.2   Opposition from Institutions and Politics

Attempts to advance justice and accountability may run afoul of institutional and political resistance. Establishing a culture of responsibility, garnering widespread support, and making sure changes are carried out successfully are all necessary to overcome opposition.

8.9.3   Global Issues' Complexity

Global problems like economic inequality, climate change, and geopolitical conflicts create complicated problems that need for coordinated efforts and creative solutions. International cooperation, multilateral agreements, and a dedication to common ideals of justice and accountability are required to address these issues.

A wide range of dynamic ideas and behaviours are included in the vision of accountability and justice with the goal of guaranteeing justice, openness, and equal treatment in a variety of settings. A complete strategy including institutional and legal frameworks, openness and public involvement, and a dedication to overcoming obstacles are needed to realise this objective. By pursuing justice and accountability, society may foster moral behaviour, foster trust, and make the world a more fair and equitable place for everyone.

8.10   Potential outcomes and impact on society

Public confidence in institutions—government, judiciary, and corporate—tends to rise when accountability and justice are executed successfully. Fairness in treatment and transparent decision-making help to create a favourable impression of these organisations, which encourages increased public trust and participation. Credible and dependable institutions are those that continuously preserve the values of justice and accountability. Their legitimacy and authority may be strengthened by this credibility, which will facilitate the effective implementation of projects and programs.

8.10.1 Enhanced Policy Effectiveness and Governance

Accountability procedures guarantee that judgements are founded on factual data, in-depth study, and careful consideration of many viewpoints. This results in more informed and efficient policymaking that takes the wants and concerns of the general public into account.

Corrupt practices and poor management are less likely when procedures and supervision are transparent. Effective resource management and allocation are essential to accomplishing policy objectives and providing public services.

8.10.2 Justice and Social Equity

A dedication to justice encourages equity and parity in the allocation of opportunities and resources. This can guarantee that everyone has access to the same opportunities and rights while also addressing underlying disparities. Reparations between criminals and victims are the main goals of restorative justice procedures. Because it addresses the underlying reasons of criminal behaviour, this strategy may aid in the healing of the community and lower recidivism rates.

8.10.3 Increased Involvement in Civic Life

People are more inclined to engage in civic duties like voting, community organising, and public debate when they see that their opinions count and that their issues are taken seriously. Increased participation like this supports democratic processes and makes citizens more knowledgeable and engaged. Communities are empowered by justice and accountability because they are provided with the means and resources to hold authorities and institutions responsible. Empowerment cultivates a feeling of accountability and ownership, resulting in communities that are more proactive and resilient.

8.10.4 Financial Gains

Investment conditions are solid and predictable when institutions are responsible and transparent. Systems that investors believe to be trustworthy and equitable are more likely to be used, which promotes economic development and growth. The expenses related to fraud, poor management, and legal conflicts are decreased when corruption and inefficiency are addressed. Both the public and commercial sectors may see considerable cost reductions via effective governance and equitable policies.

8.10.5 Difficulties and Things to Take Into Account

Established interests or organisations that profit from the existing quo may oppose efforts to establish accountability and justice. Building coalitions, using effective communication, and upholding the values of justice and honesty are all necessary to overcome this opposition.

Transparency is crucial, but security considerations also need to be balanced. One of the primary challenges that has to be carefully considered is making sure that sensitive data is safeguarded while allowing the public access to essential information. Over time, maintaining justice and accountability calls for constant dedication and watchfulness. It is essential to implement institutional reforms, cultural shifts, and ongoing assessment to guarantee the integration of these principles into social norms and practices.

A strong vision of justice and accountability has significant and far-reaching potential effects. A society that is more robust, egalitarian,

and successful is one that has more civic involvement, greater social justice, better governance, and stronger institutional trust. Even while there are difficulties along the road, the advantages of promoting justice and accountability outweigh the drawbacks, opening the door for a more equitable and responsible society.

CHAPTER NO. 09
THE SECOND COMING OF TRUMP

"As G.K. Chesterton once reflected, 'The world will never starve for want of wonders, but only for want of wonder.' The Second Coming of Trump is not just a political event but a renaissance of ideals, sparking a renewed sense of possibility and purpose in a nation yearning for profound change."

The phrase "Second Coming of Trump" refers to the expectation that Donald Trump would build on the success of his first term and return to the President of the United States in 2024. Supporters see this as a critical opportunity to revitalise the values and initiatives he promoted during his first administration. It is anticipated that upon his return, he would take up unfinished business from his first term, oppose the status quo in politics, and enact ground-breaking policies that are consistent with his vision for the United States.

Political polarisation is at its peak at this time, and Trump's followers see his return as a return to traditional values and a check on what they regard as the political elite's projected overreach. His 2024 presidential campaign is expected to rekindle the "Make America Great Again" movement by focussing on strict immigration laws, economic revitalisation, and a firm opposition to the so-called Deep State. The storyline of Trump's "Second Coming" reflects the intense desire of his supporters for a dramatic change in the course of policy as well as a strong challenge to the existing quo, laying the groundwork for a very divisive and historic election cycle.

9.1   Campaign Highlights

The Restoration Message

The core platform of the 2024 Trump campaign is "restoration," which seeks to restore the nation's economic vigour, sense of pride in its heritage, and conservative ideals to what they were before to 2016. Trump presents himself as the antidote to the policies that he and his followers believe are a mishash of bad decisions made by the previous government. This message is conveyed via speeches, advertisements, and proposed policies that emphasise rolling back regulations, reversing previous legislative actions, and upholding fundamental American values. The campaign has a strong emphasis on restoring economic growth, religious freedom, and law and order.

Plans for Economic Revival

The campaign pledges to minimise bureaucracy and government involvement in the economy. Reducing rules for companies and financial institutions is one way to promote innovation and economic progress. In an effort to encourage investment and expenditure, Trump is proposing additional tax cuts for both people and corporations. This entails growing and prolonging the tax reductions put in place during his first tenure. The campaign's main goal is to create jobs in the United States by providing incentives to businesses who choose to produce there. This include funding infrastructure initiatives and assisting sectors such as technology and energy.

Immigration Laws

Trump's campaign placed a strong emphasis on strengthening border security measures and building the wall with Mexico. This entails putting new monitoring systems into place and augmenting budget for the border patrol. The campaign advocates for the harsh enforcement of immigration regulations, which includes sanctuary city closures and the expulsion of undocumented immigrants. Protecting American employment and bolstering national security are the objectives. In an effort to draw in highly qualified people and lower the number of unlawful entries, proposals call for a merit-based immigration system that places a higher priority on credentials and abilities than family ties.

Reaction to the Deep State

According to the campaign, Trump's comeback is a fight against the "Deep State," a phrase used to characterise what he and his followers believe to be a powerful, dishonest political and administrative establishment that opposes the interests of the American people. Trump has pledged in his speech to bring corruption in the government to light and to make it more transparent. This is presented as a component of his larger plan to clear the swamp and bring responsibility back.

Bring the MAGA Movement Back

By planning sizable demonstrations, interacting with local groups, and enlisting volunteers, the initiative aims to revitalise the MAGA movement. This strategy seeks to increase fervour and momentum among Trump's supporters. Trump's campaign uses social media sites instead of conventional media outlets to reach out to people directly. This includes regular updates on social media sites like Facebook, Twitter, and Truth Social in addition to live-streamed events and interviews.

Position on Foreign Policy

Trump is a champion of renegotiating trade agreements in the best interests of US workers and companies. This entails revising agreements with important trading partners and applying tariffs to those he perceives as engaging in unfair trade practices. The campaign advocates for lessening American military participation in foreign wars in favour of bolstering national defence and making sure other countries make more contributions to their own security. Trump places a strong emphasis on a practical strategy for foreign policy that puts American interests first and lessens dependence on alliances and accords that he views as harmful.

Evaluation of the Media

The campaign keeps up its criticism of the mainstream media, charging it with disseminating false information and being biassed. This critique is intended to undermine the unfavourable media coverage of Trump and mobilise his supporters. In order to combat what they perceive to be a hostile mainstream media environment,

Trump's team concentrates on using alternative media sources, such as independent news platforms and social media.

Legal and Inquiry Difficulties

The campaign characterises continuing legal disputes and investigations as politically driven attempts to damage Trump's reputation and obstruct his bid for reelection. According to Trump's legal team and campaign, these legal challenges are a part of a larger plot to discredit him and divert attention away from his platform and policy accomplishments. The strategic elements of Trump's 2024 campaign are encapsulated in these in-depth highlights, which also show how he intends to overcome obstacles, build on prior victories, and galvanise support for a presidential comeback.

9.2   Crucial Speeches and Rallies

Key Rallies and Speeches

Re-Launch Rally in Florida (2023)

- **Location:** Miami, Florida
- **Significance:** This rally marked the official re-launch of Trump's presidential campaign. It set the tone for the campaign with a strong emphasis on the need to restore America's greatness and address the perceived failures of the current administration.
- **Highlights:** Trump articulated his vision for economic recovery, border security, and law and order. The rally featured enthusiastic crowds and was designed to energize his base and signal the start of an intense campaign.

"America First" Rally in Ohio (2024)

- **Location**: Columbus, Ohio
- **Significance**: This rally focused on Trump's economic policies and his "America First" agenda. Ohio, a key swing state, was targeted to solidify support and demonstrate Trump's ongoing relevance in critical electoral regions.
- **Highlights**: Trump detailed his plans for tax cuts, deregulation, and job creation. He also attacked the current administration's economic policies, emphasizing the need for a return to his previous administration's economic successes.

Border Security Rally in Texas (2024)

- **Location**: El Paso, Texas
- **Significance**: Texas was chosen for this rally to highlight Trump's commitment to border security and immigration reform. The event underscored his stance on building the border wall and enhancing law enforcement at the border.
- **Highlights**: Trump reiterated his promises to complete the border wall and crack down on illegal immigration. The rally featured testimonials from local officials and border patrol agents who supported his immigration policies.

"Great Awakening" Rally in Pennsylvania (2024)

- **Location**: Pittsburgh, Pennsylvania
- **Significance**: This rally focused on the "Great Awakening" theme, which Trump's campaign framed as a movement to reclaim American values and address what he describes as deep-seated corruption and overreach by the establishment.

- **Highlights**: Trump spoke about his vision for a new Golden Age and the need to confront the "Deep State." The rally was aimed at galvanizing grassroots support and rallying those disillusioned with the political establishment.

Veterans' Appreciation Rally in Michigan (2024)

- **Location**: Detroit, Michigan
- **Significance**: Held to honor military veterans and emphasize Trump's commitment to the armed forces. Michigan, another key swing state, was selected to appeal to veteran communities and patriotic voters.
- **Highlights**: Trump praised the military and highlighted his administration's achievements in defense and veterans' affairs. He promised increased support and benefits for veterans and active-duty personnel.

Economic Prosperity Speech in New York City (2024)

- **Location**: Manhattan, New York City
- **Significance**: Trump's speech in New York City was intended to showcase his economic policies and appeal to both business leaders and the general public. It aimed to contrast his vision with the current administration's economic record.
- **Highlights**: Trump laid out his plan for economic revitalization, including tax cuts, deregulation, and infrastructure investment. He criticized the current economic policies and presented his agenda as the solution for economic growth.

"Justice and Accountability" Rally in Washington, D.C. (2024)

- **Location:** Washington, D.C.
- **Significance:** This rally was held to address ongoing legal battles and the broader theme of "Justice and Accountability." It was aimed at portraying Trump as a victim of political persecution and rallying support against the perceived corruption of the establishment.
- **Highlights:** Trump defended his legal battles and criticized the investigations against him as politically motivated. He framed these issues within a larger narrative of fighting corruption and restoring justice.

Final Campaign Push Rally in Wisconsin (2024)

- **Location:** Milwaukee, Wisconsin
- **Significance:** As a key battleground state, Wisconsin was chosen for a major final push rally before the election. The event was designed to consolidate support and mobilize voters in a critical electoral state.
- **Highlights:** Trump made a final appeal to voters, summarizing his campaign's key messages and emphasizing the importance of the upcoming election. The rally featured high-energy speeches and performances aimed at maximizing voter turnout.

These rallies and speeches were pivotal in shaping Trump's 2024 campaign narrative, rallying his base, and addressing key issues. They reflect his strategic focus on core campaign themes, battleground states, and critical voter demographics.

9.3　Grassroots movements and public support

Rise of Grassroots Organizations

The 2024 Trump campaign saw a notable resurgence in grassroots activism and public support, drawing from the strategies that fueled his 2016 and 2020 campaigns. Several grassroots organizations and movements played a pivotal role in rallying support and mobilizing voters:

- **"Make America Great Again" (MAGA) Groups**: These groups, originally formed during Trump's first campaign, continued to be a significant force. They organized local events, volunteer drives, and fundraising efforts, fostering a strong network of engaged supporters.
- **"Stop the Steal" Network**: Although controversial, this network of activists focused on questioning election integrity and rallying supporters around claims of widespread election fraud. The network played a role in maintaining high levels of enthusiasm and engagement among Trump's base.
- **Local Chapters and Committees**: Across various states, local chapters of Trump's campaign worked tirelessly to organize town halls, meet-and-greet events, and rallies. These local efforts helped personalize the campaign and create a sense of community and shared purpose among supporters.

Key Grassroots Initiatives

- **Voter Registration Drives**: Grassroots organizations actively engaged in voter registration drives to expand the electorate and mobilize support for Trump. These efforts targeted swing states and traditionally Democratic strongholds, aiming to increase Republican voter turnout.

- **Social Media Campaigns**: Trump's supporters leveraged social media platforms to spread campaign messages, organize virtual events, and counteract mainstream media narratives. Hashtags like #MAGA2024 and #Trump2024 became rallying cries for online activism and support.

- **Community Outreach Programs**: Grassroots activists engaged in direct community outreach, including door-to-door canvassing, phone banking, and community events. These efforts aimed to connect with voters on a personal level and address their concerns about the state of the nation.

Public Support and Rallying Points

- **Economic Concerns**: Economic issues, including inflation and job losses, were central to Trump's appeal. Grassroots movements highlighted these concerns and positioned Trump as the solution to the nation's economic troubles.

- **Cultural and Social Issues**: Trump's stance on cultural and social issues, such as opposition to critical race theory and support for traditional values, resonated strongly with many grassroots supporters. These issues were frequently emphasized in local campaign events and media outreach.

- **Anti-Establishment Sentiment**: The anti-establishment sentiment that fueled Trump's previous campaigns remained strong. Grassroots supporters viewed Trump as a fighter against a corrupt political system, further galvanizing their support and activism.

Impact and Challenges

- **Increased Voter Turnout**: The grassroots movements contributed to increased voter turnout in key battleground states. This turnout was crucial in maintaining Trump's competitive position in the 2024 election.
- **Challenges with Division**: While grassroots support was robust, the campaign faced challenges with internal divisions and controversies. The persistence of claims about election fraud and the contentious nature of the political environment sometimes created friction within the movement.
- **Media Coverage**: The media's portrayal of grassroots efforts varied, with some outlets highlighting the enthusiasm and organization of Trump's supporters, while others criticized the movement's tactics and narratives.

Overall, grassroots movements and public support played a critical role in shaping the 2024 Trump campaign. The combination of organized activism, strategic outreach, and addressing key voter concerns helped drive the campaign's momentum and sustain its appeal among a significant portion of the electorate.

9.4 The Near-Death Trump Assassination Attempt: A Miracle in Modern Times

The almost fatal attempt on the life of former President Donald Trump remains one of the most momentous and terrible incidents of our time. This episode, which happened during his 2024 election campaign, was not just a political figure's assault; rather, it was a significant moment that many have interpreted as a sign from God and a turning point in contemporary history.

The assassination attempt on President Trump was a well-thought-out inside operation, carried out by people with access to critical information and a thorough grasp of security procedures. The scheme, which sought to remove Trump and thwart his political comeback, was set up for eventual success. The audience, however, saw a remarkable change of events that transformed what seemed to be a moment of terrible inevitability into one of miraculous survival.

The effort proved to be a remarkable escape for Trump, who was on the verge of imminent death. Unforeseen events happened, foiling the opponents' goals despite the attack's accuracy and forethought. Many think that this episode proves there is a greater force protecting Trump in a way that can only be characterised as supernatural.

In addition to captivating the public, this incredible survival has strengthened the belief that Trump's leadership has a spiritual component. This incident confirms for many of Trump's fans the belief that he is a divinely appointed leader shielded from the evil plans of his opponents. The idea that a miracle saved Trump's life has stoked a story about a spiritual conflict between good and evil, in which Trump stands for the forces of truth and light. As more people start to see Trump's leadership in a new, heavenly light, support for him has increased in the wake of the assassination attempt. His supporters now feel even more certain that he is meant to lead and that his work is far from done. The episode has also stirred public opinion, exposing the strength and tenacity of his movement and underlining the extent some would go to in order to stop him from regaining power.

The tale surrounding Donald Trump's near-death assassination attempt is spiritually significant in addition to being a political thriller. It has bolstered the determination of Trump's fans and confirmed the idea that there is a higher power at work in his administration. This incident will be remembered when history is written, not just for its dramatic quality but also for helping to shape the narrative of a presidency characterised by both supernatural and human intervention.

9.4.1   The Plot: An Inside Job

The Trump assassination plot was a well-planned and terrifying inside operation. It involves people with access to confidential information and in-depth understanding of security details. Because the attackers were positioned deliberately to take advantage of gaps in security, the attempt's success was almost certain. This degree of insider participation suggested a complex conspiracy with perhaps deep roots in intelligence and political circles that had a stake in keeping Trump from winning back the presidency. To ensure maximum effect and turmoil, the plan to remove Trump at a high-profile event was painstakingly prepared. The attackers expected a decisive move that would happen quickly and without chance of mistake. The plot's blatant disregard for the law highlighted the desperate efforts of those who wanted to remove Trump from office in order to achieve their goals.

9.4.2   The Miraculous Intervention

Even though the scheme was executed with deadly accuracy, an amazing and unexpected sequence of events happened. The assassination attempt failed due to a sequence of miscalculations and unanticipated interventions that occurred at a key time. For example, Trump's timetable had a little but significant delay that changed the timeframe, and the attackers' equipment suddenly broke down, making it impossible to carry out the operation as planned. Many have seen these apparently random events as supernatural interventions that stopped what would have otherwise looked to be an inevitable disaster.

Witnesses and security staff attested to a tangible feeling of divine intervention, because events beyond human control were pivotal to the conclusion. The story that Trump had been spared by a higher force swiftly gained traction, and his fans firmly believed this to be true. The belief that Trump's life is under supernatural protection and that his destiny transcends common political conflicts has been strengthened by this episode.

9.4.3   The Aftermath: A Surge in Support

The attempted assassination had immediate and significant repercussions. The event gained widespread attention from the media, who covered it in great detail. Some media sources emphasised the political ramifications and the conspiracy probe, while others emphasised how amazing Trump's survival is. The audience was enthralled with this twin story of a supernatural miracle and a political scheme. Already fervently loyal supporters of Trump, they saw the event as validation of their conviction in his unique position. The notion that he was shielded by supernatural powers struck a deep chord, sparking an upsurge in popular support. Attendance at public events like as rallies surged, with many participants voicing their conviction that Trump was a chosen leader who was meant to battle evil. Rather than undermining Trump's standing, the attempt on his life served to further solidify the image of him as a hero and a martyr against a corrupt and evil system.

9.4.4   The Spiritual Aspect

It is impossible to overestimate the assassination attempt's spiritual component. Many others see the incident as a sign of a greater cosmic conflict between good and evil. Trump's miraculous survival is seen as evidence that he is on a divine mission and is shielded from harm by powers that are beyond our understanding. The current environment, in which many people believe that there is a moral and spiritual crisis facing the globe and that Trump has been selected as the leader to bring back justice and order, has strengthened this idea. Discussions about the nature of the conflict being fought not merely in the political sphere but also in the spiritual one—have also gained prominence as a result of the tragedy. The talk of a spiritual conflict between the forces of good and truth and the forces of evil and deceit has become more prevalent. In this view, the attempt on Trump's life is seen as a physical embodiment of this conflict, and his survival serves as a sign of optimism and the final victory of good over evil.

9.4.5   Implications for the Future

The near-death encounter has significant future ramifications for Trump and the larger political scene. It has strengthened his base of support, given his campaign impetus, and established him as a person of almost legendary tenacity. For those who consider themselves as part of a historical movement towards a new period of justice and truth, the belief in a divine component to his administration adds another level of drive.

The narrative of the attempted murder of Donald Trump is one of mystery, faith, and providence. This is a moment that touches on higher issues of destiny and divine purpose, rising beyond the banal features of politics. This episode will surely be regarded as a turning point in the story as it unfolds, one that not only tested the boundaries of human cruelty but also demonstrated the possibility of supernatural intervention and the lasting strength of faith.

9.5 Trump's Reaction to the Assassination Attempt: A Statement of Resilience and Faith

Trump's Response to the Attempt on His Life: A Deep Introspection and Rekindled Hope

Following the almost disastrous attempt on his life, Donald Trump gave a speech to the country and the globe in which he combined sombre introspection, unwavering determination, and a reaffirmation of his goal. The situation was obviously serious, and Trump's answer was a political and personal declaration with strong religious undertones that reaffirmed his dedication to his followers and the American people as a whole.

9.5.1 Recognition of the Incident

In his opening remarks, President Trump addressed the assassination attempt directly, calling it a "cowardly and treacherous act" carried out by those who want to subvert the will of the American people. He conveyed his sincere gratitude for his security detail's and law enforcement's prompt efforts in neutralising the danger and averting a potentially disastrous consequence. When expressing the gravity of the incident, Trump did not hold back, characterising it as "a stark reminder of the dangers we face from those who oppose our mission to restore America's greatness."

9.5.2 Expression of Faith and Gratitude

Trump discussed the miraculous aspect of his survival in a very moving section of his speech. He described how the attempt to kill him failed against all difficulties, and he attributed his escape to "divine intervention." In addition to his security detail, he sent his sincere appreciation to "the guiding hand of God." Deeply spiritual conviction permeated Trump's statement, "There is no other explanation for the way things unfolded." It was a miracle. It was evidence that we are headed in the right direction and that our cause is just. This episode simply confirms my opinion that we are engaged in a spiritual conflict in addition to a political one, which I have long held."

9.5.3 Reassurance to Supporters and Call for Unity

Turning to face his fans, Trump thanked them from the bottom of his heart for their continuous support and prayers. He assured them that he was not discouraged while acknowledging the dread and uncertainty the assassination attempt had surely induced. He addressed the millions of Americans who had supported him personally, stating, "I appreciate all of your support. Your support in the form of love, prayers, and faith in our cause is what keeps me going. If we work together, we can not only withstand these assaults but also come out stronger and closer to one another."

9.5.4 Condemnation of the Attack and Commitment to Justice

Trump denounced the attack's perpetrators while raising the possibility of a wider conspiracy and calling it a "inside job" involving people from both within and outside the government. He said that "no one is above the law" and that betrayal and acts of violence of this kind will not go unpunished. He also promised to bring those guilty to justice. In order to determine the whole scope of the scheme and make sure that everyone involved is held responsible, he promised to collaborate closely with law enforcement and intelligence organisations.

9.5.5 Reaffirmation of His Mission

Trump said in a combative manner that the attempt on his life had strengthened rather than diminished his determination. He reaffirmed his dedication to the key tenets of his campaign and his outlook for the future of the United States. "This attempt on my life was not just an attack on me, but an attack on the movement we have built together," he said. "It was an attack on the values we hold dear: freedom, justice, and the right of every American to live in a country where their voice is heard and respected."

9.5.6 Spiritual Overtones and Call to Action

Lastly, Trump explained the episode in terms of a broader spiritual framework. Speaking of the continuous "war between good and evil," he positioned himself and his allies as champions of righteousness. Invoking images from the Book of Revelation, he implied that tremendous disclosures were taking place in this century and that the powers of evil were coming to light. He said, "We are living in the middle of a tremendous awakening that will usher in a new golden era for America—a period of wealth, peace, and rekindled faith. God is on our side, and we shall win with Him, thus the powers of evil will not prevail."

Trump urged his fans to be alert and involved as he ended his address with a call to action. He promised to fight for the principles they held dear and begged them to keep doing so. "We're not going to be quiet. We are not going to be scared. We will succeed in making America great once again by working together, and this will be a historic triumph." In response to the attempted assassination, Trump expressed a potent blend of gratitude, resistance, and fervour for his religion. He presented the event as a turning point in the continuous conflict between light and darkness as well as a personal battle. His message was quite clear: the attempt on his life had only strengthened his resolve to fight for what he believed to be the correct cause and goal. It served as a rallying cry for his followers, strengthening their faith in Trump as a divinely inspired leader against the powers of evil and corruption. A Strong and Resilient Applicant

Donald Trump is emerging as a strong contender who is ready to energise a sizable and ardent constituency as the 2024 U.S. presidential election draws near. Numerous polls and political assessments indicate that Trump's impact is still strong, which has important ramifications for the election and the future of the United States of America. Many consider his prospective return to the White House as a turning point in the course of the country as well as the perpetuation of his political legacy.

9.6　　A Resilient and Powerful Candidacy

A number of important elements will contribute to Trump's popularity in 2024. First of all, a sizable portion of the American population still finds resonance in his own brand of populism, especially among people who feel marginalised or abandoned by the political elite. Known as the "forgotten man and woman," this demographic sees in Trump a champion who addresses their issues with national sovereignty, cultural identity, and economic stability. This base's steadfast devotion is reinforced by Trump's capacity to engage supporters with his straightforward and unvarnished communication style, often eschewing conventional media outlets in favour of social media and in-person events.

One of the most important aspects of Trump's compelling campaign is his firm position on subjects that his followers find very important. Strict immigration laws, economic protectionism, a strong military, and a foreign policy that puts "America First" are all highlighted in his agenda. In the face of both local and international issues, these positions—which were essential to his 2016 campaign—have not only stayed the same but have significantly sharpened. For example, people from the working class who have been negatively impacted by globalisation find Trump's economic platform, which calls for cutting trade imbalances and reintroducing manufacturing jobs to the United States, appealing.

Trump's appeal also originates from his reputation as a political outsider who isn't afraid to take on established political and administrative structures. He has gained a reputation as a disruptor because to his criticism of the "Deep State" and his combative style with the mainstream media. Many of his fans believe that disruption is essential to overcoming governmental corruption and deadlock. His repeated claims that his administration is protected by God, which appeal to a sizable section of his religiously driven supporters, serve to further cement this image.

9.6.1 The Impact on America's Global Standing

Trump's leadership style and policy goals are anticipated to have a significant impact on America's status internationally should he win the 2024 election. Trump's foreign policy strategy is a departure from multilateralism, as seen by his preference for bilateral deals and attention to national interests. A more forceful US presence on the international scene is suggested by his administration's focus on "peace through strength" and transactional approach to international affairs. This may result in harder postures against foes like China and Iran as well as deeper military ties with nations ready to support American interests. Renegotiating trade agreements and reducing American participation in foreign organisations that, in his opinion, do not advance American interests are likely to continue throughout a second term of office for Trump. When both friends and foes of the United States navigate a more unpredictable and forceful foreign policy, this might further polarise views of America around the world. But these steps are considered by many of Trump's followers as essential remedies to decades of what they see to be American decline under earlier administrations.

9.6.2 Economic Vision and Domestic Prosperity

Reviving American industry and lowering reliance on other countries are at the core of Trump's domestic economic agenda. Tax reductions, deregulation, and incentives for domestic manufacturing are anticipated to be the main focusses of his programs. Trump wants to boost employment growth and draw investment by making the climate more business-friendly, especially for the industrial and energy industries. This economic plan promises a strong economy with more employment possibilities and greater incomes in an effort to appeal to both the corporate community and the working class.

A key component of Trump's economic policy strategy is his adamant opposition to illegal immigration, which he claims drives down wages and puts a burden on public services. Trump portrays himself as a champion of American employment and the country's sovereignty by pushing for tighter immigration laws and border security measures. Even though it is divisive, this position is essential to his appeal to those who are worried about both cultural cohesiveness and economic security.

9.6.3   Cultural and Social Implications

Trump's reelection may deepen the country's already-existing political and social divisions on a cultural level. His language often plays on conservative ideals, such as a heavy focus on law and order, resistance to progressive social reforms, and support for the Second Amendment. This paints Trump as a champion of traditional American values, appealing to a sizable segment of the voter that is disenchanted with the fast pace of societal change. Meanwhile, there has been a lot of criticism of Trump's divisive demeanour and contentious remarks, especially from liberal and progressive organisations. Strong political and cultural conflicts have characterised his administration, with racial relations, women's rights, and free expression often at the centre. These disputes may become worse if Trump is given a second term because of his administration's pursuit of conservative objectives that go against progressive conventions.

9.6.4   The Future of American Politics

In the long run, the political climate in America is probably going to be significantly impacted by Trump's possible return to the White House. His ability to energise a sizable and fervent voting base has shown the effectiveness of populism and transformed the Republican Party in his image. This change may result in a political climate that is more ideologically unified but also more divisive, further widening the gulf between Trump's partisans and critics. the possibility of a Trump administration in 2024 marks a pivotal moment in American history. His formidable campaign, emphasised by steady backing from a wide constituency, a distinct policy outlook, and a firm position on both domestic and foreign matters, implies that his impact on the future of the country is far from concluded. There is no doubting that Trump will have a significant influence on America's political, economic, and cultural domains, regardless of one's perspective—that of a polarising character or a savior. With Trump's leadership providing a clear route towards a vision of

America that prioritises power, sovereignty, and a return to traditional values, the country finds itself at a crossroads as the election draws near.

CHAPTER NO. 10
THE SPIRITUAL BATTLE – SIGNS AND PROPHECIES

10.1 The Symbolic Opening Ceremony of the Olympics

Olympic opening ceremonies are significant events that are often lavishly staged and full of artistic and cultural expression. The last event, however, caused a great deal of controversy and discussion because some people saw occult or demonic undertones in its images. There was a lot of conjecture on the motivations behind the creative decisions due to the usage of eerie, enigmatic symbols and dramatic presentations. Many people saw these aspects as signals reflecting deeper, maybe dangerous tales rather than just works of art.

Critics and onlookers drew attention to certain symbols, such mysterious rituals, occult figures, and apparently esoteric themes, implying that they were intentional depictions of a metaphysical conflict between good and evil. This interpretation gained popularity, especially among those who think that there is a worldwide war between good and evil, and that the opening ceremony was an obvious way for darker powers to show their support. Defenders of the ritual, on the other side, said that the picture was entirely artistic and intended to evoke contemplation while reflecting difficult topics like human struggle, perseverance, and light triumphing over darkness. They stressed that, depending on one's viewpoint, these readings might differ greatly and were subjective.

The responses from the public and media were divisive. While some viewers were uncomfortable and worried that the ceremony had veered too close to the macabre, others were appreciative of the audacious artistic choice and saw it as an effective narrative technique. This difference in public perception emphasises how the event affects the communal awareness, where art and symbolism converge with individual convictions and society anxieties. The Olympic opening ceremony was a significant cultural artefact that sparked discussion and introspection on more profound spiritual and existential issues, demonstrating the influence of symbolism in modern culture.

10.2   Analysis of the Ceremony's Imagery

The mysterious and thought-provoking graphics of the Olympic opening ceremony generated a great deal of curiosity and discussion. The visuals of the event were full of symbolic components, which many saw as an expression of a deeper spiritual story, emphasising in particular a supposed conflict between good and evil. This essay explores the many meanings and wider societal ramifications of the intricate tapestry of symbols and themes used in the ritual.

The depictions of gloomy, shadowy characters and occult symbols, which dominated the ceremony's style, were at the center of the debate. A feeling of mysticism and otherworldliness was produced by the employment of veiled figures, mysterious sigils, and ceremonial situations. Some observers saw these components as underlying messages rather than just creative flourishes. Some saw the existence of these symbols as proof of occult influence, implying that a clandestine spiritual conflict was taking place on a worldwide scale. As a result, the event was seen as a ceremonial performance that fit with esoteric customs that many associate with a conflict between light and evil. The music and dance added to the ominous ambiance of the event. A sombre, discordant soundtrack accompanied the performers' careful, almost ritualistic accuracy in movement. There are many who claim that the event was intended to instill anxiety or disquiet because of the uncomfortable atmosphere created by this creative direction decision. Critics saw the purposeful choice of such a gloomy topic as an effort to gently nudge viewers' subconscious, pulling them into a story of turmoil and strife. According to this perspective, the event was seen as a symbolic portrayal of the forces of evil trying to take control of the collective consciousness, supporting the notion of a spiritual conflict.

Still, there were differing interpretations of the ceremony's iconography. Some perceived it as a sinister exhibition of spirituality, while others saw it as a daring demonstration of contemporary creative inventiveness. According to this interpretation, the ritual pushed the bounds of creative expression by including dark themes and occult symbolism. One interpretation of the enigmatic images and mystical features is that they represent the unknowns of the cosmos and the hidden facets of human psychology. According to this interpretation, the event was a confrontation with the intricacies of life and the human condition rather than an endorsement of darkness.

Furthermore, a few cultural analysts proposed that the ritual was a statement on current international affairs. The contrast between the bright and dark components can stand for the duality of optimism and despair in the modern society.

The final appearance of light might represent the victory of justice, truth, and human resiliency, while the gloomy images can represent the battles against injustice, inequity, and corruption. This story is consistent with the more general concept of a spiritual awakening, sometimes known as a "Great Awakening," in which the revelation of latent truths causes a general realisation and metamorphosis. To sum up, the imagery used in the opening ceremony was a sophisticated combination of symbols that could be interpreted in a variety of ways. The event was successful in drawing attention from all around the globe, regardless of whether one views it as a literal portrayal of a spiritual conflict, a daring creative endeavour, or a meditation on social issues. It acted as a potent cultural relic, inspiring contemplation on the nature of symbols, the influence of the media, and the continuous conflict between forces that are considered to be good and evil.

10.3   The Spiritual Battle Context

The idea that forces of good and evil are always at war in a realm that exists outside of the material world is the foundation of the notion of a spiritual conflict. According to this viewpoint, these invisible spiritual struggles are often reflected in events that occur in the material world. The notion has been a major issue in many philosophical and theological traditions, but it is most prominently seen in Christianity, where it is expressed in the biblical story of God and Satan, or light and darkness, at war.

This spiritual conflict is seen as being more apparent and powerful in light of recent events, such as the Olympic Games' symbolic opening ceremony and the attempted murder of former President Trump. Many people see these episodes as part of a greater cosmic conflict. The eerie and mysterious imagery of the ceremony, together with Trump's escape from an attempted murder, are seen as indications of this continuing spiritual conflict. The ceremony's ominous symbolism is seen to symbolise the forces of evil seeking to exert their influence, while Trump's miraculous protection is understood to be proof of divine intervention and the existence of a higher, kind power defending justice and the truth.

Those who hold the belief that there is a "Great Awakening," during which time secrets are being exposed and people are becoming more conscious of the spiritual forces affecting the material world, will find great resonance in this story. This ideology holds that the fight for humanity's soul and the revelation of long-hidden evil practices characterise the contemporary period. The "era of revelations," which alludes to the last book of the Bible, Revelation, is said to be the period when all secrets will be revealed and a final judgement will follow.

The murder attempt on Trump is seen as more than simply a political act; it is seen as a part of this spiritual fight, especially during this turbulent election season. Supporters see Trump's survival and ongoing political career as a symbol of good triumphing over evil and his position as crucial in bringing in a new era. The idea that notable people and events are not just coincidences but rather are a part of a divine plan that is unfolding in accordance with a greater cosmic purpose supports this point of view.

Additionally, this spiritual backdrop is connected to more general eschatological themes, such the anticipated "Golden Age" or "new heaven and new earth." This religion holds that the spiritual war's conclusion will bring about an unparalleled era of harmony, wealth, and peace known as the "Golden Age." It is believed that after awakening to spiritual truths and rejecting the powers of evil, mankind will live in accordance with divine principles throughout this period. Freedom, fairness, and prosperity will be the hallmarks of a reformed society brought about by the rejuvenated intellect of an awakened spirit. The idea of the spiritual fight offers a framework for looking beyond politics and social processes to comprehend current events. It asserts that the forces of good and evil are clearly defined at this critical juncture in human history, and the result of this fight will dictate how history develops in the future. This story teaches moral clarity and alertness by claiming that, even in the face of seeming chaos and strife, a divine order will finally triumph, meaning that "God wins."

The Miraculous Protection of Trump

Donald Trump's escape from what many believe to be an attempted murder is sometimes presented as a miraculous occurrence with great spiritual significance. This interpretation stems from the idea that these kinds of events have deeper, often supernatural implications and are not just coincidences.

10.4.1 The Incident's Nature

A big and concerning development in the backdrop of the 2024 presidential campaign was the attempted murder of Donald Trump.

Through political and spiritual views, the attack's details—how it was stopped, the events surrounding it, and Trump's first response—are examined. Focusing on elements that appear to contradict expectations or conventional explanations—like unanticipated interventions, the specifics of the attack's failure, or Trump's unharmed survival in spite of the seriousness of the threat—highlights the miraculous quality of this protection.

10.4.2 Symbolism and Interpretation

Trump's survival is often seen by supporters and pundits as a sign of divine intervention or favor. According to this perspective, Trump's remarkable occurrence cannot be explained by random chance; rather, it must be linked to a greater force that is actively maintaining and directing his fate. According to this view, Trump's survival proves that he is a part of a greater, divine plan, which is consistent with more general religious ideas about divine protection and purpose.

10.4.3 Political and Spiritual Importance

The idea of supernatural defence combines with political narratives to present Trump as a key player in a spiritual conflict between good and evil. His followers see his sustained participation in politics in spite of grave threats as proof of the backing of a higher power and the larger fight against evil powers. According to this perspective, his survival proves his tenacity and highlights his supposed contribution to facing and vanquishing systematic evil.

10.4.4 Wider Consequences

Understanding present events is further complicated by the idea in miraculous protection. It implies that social and political conflicts are mirror images of a greater cosmic conflict in which specific individuals are seen as proxies for more expansive spiritual forces. According to this perspective, Trump's survival not only represents a personal win but also the victory of good over evil and confirms the idea that divine justice will finally triumph.

10.4.5 Effect on Public Opinion

Public opinion and the political environment are influenced by the belief that Trump is providing miraculous protection. It strengthens the belief among Trump's supporters that he is a specially selected individual and paints his opponents as members of the forces resisting divine will. Voters who see the assault as a part of a bigger conflict with existential consequences may become more supportive of the political cause and get mobilized by this viewpoint. Many see Trump's miraculous protection as a sign of divine favor and intervention when seen through a spiritual perspective. This concept affects public perception as well as the political dynamics of the 2024 election by placing Trump within a broader cosmic narrative of good against evil.

10.5   The Assassination Attempt

An attempt was attempted on the life of former President Donald Trump on a significant day in the 2024 election campaign. There was heightened political tension and scrutiny at the time of this episode. Before inflicting any fatal damage, the attacker—whose identity and motivations were swiftly revealed—was apparently caught. The attempt's immediate details—how it developed, the security precautions put in place, and the prompt action taken by law enforcement—became the subject of extensive media attention and widespread public concern.

10.5.1 Context and Intention

Investigating the perpetrator's past and intentions is necessary to comprehend the attack's context. Knowing the attacker's background, connections, and any previous threats or warnings is essential to understanding the motivations for the attempt. This section delves into the wider political and social milieu that might have impacted the assault, including any radical beliefs or grievances directed at Trump.

10.5.2 Quick Reaction

The attempt at assassination was met with a prompt and comprehensive reaction. Law police, emergency medical services, and security professionals moved swiftly to secure the situation and provide Trump urgent help. Here is a description of the actions taken, which included providing emergency medical attention and quickly apprehending the assailant. This section also discusses the steps taken to guarantee Trump's safety after the event, as well as his first public remarks.

10.5.3 Public Reaction and Media Coverage

The way the assassination attempt was portrayed in the media and how the people responded afterwards greatly influenced the story that was told about it. The tragedy was continuously covered by media sources, including comments, analysis, and updates. Public responses, such as astonishment, support, or condemnation, show how the incident has affected society as a whole. This section looks at how the public's reaction and the media's interpretation of the incident affected how people saw the assault and how it affected the election.

10.5.4 Interpretations that are Thematic and Symbolic

Following the attempted murder, a number of symbolic and thematic interpretations surfaced. Numerous advocates and analysts saw the incident as more than just an assault; rather, they regarded it as an expression of a more significant ideological or spiritual conflict. This viewpoint often presents the assault as a cosmic conflict between good and evil, and it interprets Trump's survival as evidence of divine favor or protection. This section examines the ramifications of different interpretations for Trump's campaign and public perception.

10.5.5 Election-Related Implications

The attempted assassination had a big impact on the 2024 election campaign. It heightened political tensions, impacting both campaign dynamics and voter opinion. Trump and his associates used the effort to amplify their claim that they are the targets of hostile forces and to rally support. This section examines the ways in which the attack affected voter behaviour, campaign tactics, and the overall election environment.

10.5.6 Extended Consequences

Beyond the immediate emotions and ramifications, the assassination attempt has long-term impacts. This covers how it affects Trump's campaign path, high-profile figure security procedures, and the larger political conversation. The event could have influenced recurring themes in the election by influencing public opinion and political narratives in the months before the vote. The attempt on Donald Trump's life during the 2024 presidential campaign was a significant incident with intricate details. Its effects rippled throughout the political landscape, impacting public opinion, media attention, and the general electoral dynamic.

10.6 The Revelation Era

An idea from eschatological and spiritual settings, the Era of Revelations is especially associated with the last book of the Bible, the Book of Revelation. This age is marked by cosmic conflicts between forces of good and evil, the profound discovery of secret truths, and pervasive corruption. It marks a time when long-hidden truths and secrets come to light, bringing about profound shifts in both society norms and human awareness.

10.6.1 Exposing Concealed Realities

Bringing to light what has been concealed or kept out of the public eye is a fundamental idea of the Age of Revelations. This is a time of exposes exposing systematic corruption, hidden truths, and manipulations by influential people. The idea is that reality, which was formerly hidden or misrepresented, is now coming to light, often in shocking and convincing ways. Political scandals, the covert plans of powerful organisations, or even spiritual revelations that defy accepted wisdom might all be part of this revelation.

10.6.2 The Aesthetic Aspect

The Age of Revelations is associated with a period of profound spiritual awakening and moral reckoning, both theologically and spiritually. It fits perfectly with apocalyptic concepts in which a fresh beginning anticipates the end of an age. This time span is often used to describe a spiritual conflict between forces of good and evil, light and dark. This time of cleansing and metamorphosis is symbolised by the Book of Revelation, which contains powerful images of cosmic combat and divine judgement. Believers see this period as a summons to moral rectitude and spiritual preparation in anticipation of a future new age marked by divine justice and regeneration.

10.6.3 The Effect on Politics and Society

The Revelations Era may have a significant influence on society. When institutional confidence is undermined by the discovery of concealed realities, there may be a generalised sense of disappointment and demands for change. Demands for accountability resulting from uncovered corruption or dishonesty may put political systems under pressure. Public awareness often shifts throughout this time, leading individuals to reevaluate their values, beliefs, and allegiances. Leaders and political groups that support change and are in line with the new realities may become more well-known.

10.6.4 Cultural and Media Interpretations

Narratives in culture and the media also reference the Era of Revelations. Themes of revelation, metamorphosis, and the conflict between good and evil are often included in literature, films, and media coverage. This cultural contemplation heightens the impression that one is living in a momentous historical or spiritual period. Exposing scandals, drawing attention to contradictions, or contextualising events within a transformational or apocalyptic narrative are some of the possible foci of media coverage.

10.6.5 Getting Ready for the Future

Preparing for what comes next is a concentration that runs parallel to the disclosures. It's common to see the Age of Revelations as a transitional time leading up to a "Golden Age" or era of restored peace and prosperity. Spiritual preparedness, social changes, and a move towards more open and moral government are all part of this preparation. It is believed that this era's conclusion would bring about a fairer and enlightened society where injustices from the past are made right and a peaceful new order is formed. The revelation of secret truths, spiritual awakening, and social upheaval characterised the Era of Revelations as a revolutionary time. It represents a period of significant transition, both materially and spiritually, preparing the way for a revitalized and more enlightened society.

10.7   The Judgment and the Golden Age

The ideas of the Golden Age and Judgement stand for two interrelated stages in a revolutionary story that is often tied to eschatological and spiritual frameworks. These concepts describe a process wherein the accumulation of historical wrongs ushers in a new period of wealth and enlightenment.

10.7.1 The verdict

The Judgement phase is a time of reckoning during which people assess the deeds of individuals, organisations, and communities. This is seen as a moment when cosmic or divine justice is carried out in a multitude of religious and spiritual traditions. Addressing the injustices, corruption, and moral failings that have accrued over time is the goal of this Judgement. It entails a thorough analysis of previous choices and behaviours, which results in responsibility and repercussions. In order to make room for a fresh start, the Judgement process often aims to purge society of its moral and ethical transgressions.

10.7.2 The Shift

There is a transitional phase that comes after the Judgement phase, which is characterised by major shifts and disruptions. As current structures and processes are demolished or reconstructed, this period may be turbulent. Reevaluating leadership, institutions, and ideals are all part of the shift, which often necessitates major social and individual changes. This is a time of great struggle and conflict as new paradigms start to develop and the established methods are questioned.

10.7.3 The Age of Plenty

The transformation process culminates in the Golden Age. It is pictured as a time after the tribulations of Judgement that is marked by extreme peace, harmony, and wealth. The injustices and corruptions of the past are made right in this new period, resulting in a peaceful and educated community. The focus placed on ideals like justice, honesty, and the welfare of the group characterises this era. Technological, cultural, and spiritual developments are often associated with the Golden Age, which fosters an atmosphere that allows people and society to flourish in previously unheard-of ways.

10.7.4 A Reimagined World

The world is said to be regenerated and enhanced during the Golden Age as a result of the lessons learnt during the Judgement period. It symbolizes a new beginning where the errors of the past are fixed and a more just and peaceful society is founded. As the foundation for a happy future, this era is marked by optimism, growth, and a focus on communal welfare. To sum up, the framework of Judgement and Golden Age describes a revolutionary path from responsibility and reckoning to a new period of peace and prosperity. It illustrates how history is cyclical and how significant change has the power to bring about regeneration and progress.

10.8 Getting Ready for the Future

Imagining and actively directing the course of society, government, and personal lives in reaction to new developments and predicted shifts is part of being future-ready. This stage, which often comes after major upheavals or life-changing events, is essential to guaranteeing a seamless transition into a more hopeful and stable period.

10.8.1 Expecting Difficulties

To begin planning for the future, one must first identify probable obstacles. This entails determining and assessing any barriers that could result from changes in the political, economic, social, or environmental spheres. Through comprehension of these obstacles, communities and individuals may develop plans to reduce hazards and handle any disturbances. The creation of backup plans and the distribution of resources to deal with unanticipated problems are made possible by this proactive strategy.

10.8.2 Accepting Ingenuity

In order to be ready for the future, innovation is essential. Accepting novel concepts, approaches, and technology may spur development and adaptability. This entails making investments in innovations like digital transformation, sustainable technology, and fresh methods of problem-solving. Promoting innovation and flexibility guarantees that communities are able to take advantage of new possibilities and adjust efficiently to changing conditions.

10.8.3 Developing Hardiness

To build resilience, systems and institutions must be strengthened so they can face and overcome adversity. This entails guaranteeing strong infrastructure, bolstering social support systems, and improving economic stability. Developing abilities that will be useful in the future, supporting lifelong learning, and promoting personal and communal flexibility are all included in the concept of resilience. In times of transition, a resilient society is better able to withstand disturbances and preserve stability.

10.8.4 Encouraging Cooperation

Working together across all levels and sectors is crucial to be ready for the future. Involving stakeholders from the public sector, business, academic community, and civil society guarantees that a variety of viewpoints are taken into account and that inclusive and practical solutions are produced. Working together may result in the development of all-encompassing plans, creative fixes, and pooled resources, which can improve society's overall readiness and flexibility.

10.8.5 Leadership with Vision

Lastly, visionary leadership plays a crucial role in directing future-focused efforts. A clear and exciting future vision from a leader

inspires stakeholders and helps to coordinate efforts. They are essential in determining priorities, distributing funds, and promoting an innovative and flexible culture. To put it simply, future-proofing entails foreseeing difficulties, welcoming innovation, building resilience, encouraging teamwork, and exhibiting visionary leadership. All of these factors work together to make everyone's future more affluent and safe.

CONCLUSION

onald J. Trump has had a significant and lasting impact on American politics and culture as we come to the end of our analysis of the Trump period. "Unprecedented" has attempted to encapsulate the spirit of this turbulent time, characterised by abrupt changes, divisive discussions, and profound cultural developments. The path from the unexpected success in the 2016 election to the contentious 2020 contest and the current excitement around the 2024 contest illustrates a country at a crossroads, debating its identity and course for the future.

Bold initiatives, unconventional tactics, and a direct challenge to the accepted conventions of political discourse defined Trump's administration. Supporters hail his administration's accomplishments as first steps towards bringing back American greatness, including tax changes, deregulation, and a strong economic agenda. In the meanwhile, his tough positions on trade and immigration, along with his combative foreign policy style, sparked intense support as well as fierce criticism.

The idea of the "Deep State" and the conviction in a covert network of powerful bureaucrats and elites working against the will of the people are fundamental to Trump's story. Many people who felt marginalised and mistrusted by established institutions found resonance in this viewpoint. The period saw a notable movement towards alternative media sources and a rising scepticism of conventional narratives, coupled with a media landscape accused of bias and inaccuracy.

Deep differences and a further test of the country's endurance were revealed by the COVID-19 epidemic. Important turning points that altered the political landscape were how the crisis was handled, the subsequent public health measures, and the effect on the 2020 election. The severity of the national split was highlighted by the events leading up to the election, such as the claims of fraud and the Capitol breach on January 6th.

The 2024 election is rapidly approaching, and speculation about Trump's possible comeback to politics is causing both excitement and fear. For others, the "Great Awakening" and the idea of a "Golden Age" provide promise for a better future characterised by harmony, wealth, and peace within a revitalized moral and spiritual framework. However, there are still issues, including as the ongoing resistance from the so-called Deep State and the wider socioeconomic divisions that continue to influence the discourse in the country. The book's focus on the almost fatal assault on Trump's life serves as a sobering reminder of the high stakes and unstable character of this time. It represents the perils and tenacity of a movement that believes it is up against strong, often invisible forces. This occurrence, which presents Trump as a leader shielded by providence for a cause higher than politics, has strengthened the notion among many of his fans that there is a divine component to Trump's position in American history.

"Unprecedented" is a contemplation on a pivotal period in American history as well as a history of a president. It aims to provide a thorough and nuanced explanation of the factors at work, the difficulties encountered, and the possible directions to take. The movement started by Donald J. Trump and his legacy will surely continue to influence American history as the country navigates this complicated and ever-changing environment. Trump's influence is proof of the lasting value of democratic participation and the dynamic American experiment, regardless of whether one views him as a disruptor or a deliverer.